womanhood

HOW TO RECLAIM YOUR IDENTITY AND REACH YOUR TRUE POTENTIAL

Joanna Lambe

Forward Thinking Publishing

First edition published 2024

Published by Forward Thinking Publishing

Text Copyright © Joanna Lambe

Photo credit Aga Mortlock Photography

Model Zoe Lambe

The moral rights of the author have been asserted.

The information contained in this book is intended to be educational and not as a substitute for financial planning. This information should not replace consultation with a competent financial professional. The content of this book is intended to be used as an adjunct to a rational and responsible programme prescribed by a financial professional. The author and publisher are in no way liable for any misuse of the materials.

A catalogue record of this book is available from the British Library.

ISBN: 978-1-916764-02-6

Published by Forward Thinking Publishing

Contents

Introduction

WHEN I WAS REMINDED recently that 'the personal is political' by Dr Francesca Berry, we discussed the role of women in society, at a bar. This arena would have been out of bounds for women in the past, as the only women allowed in bars then were there to 'serve and soothe' men.

So after speaking late into the night about our experiences as women today, this random meeting, along with inspiration from many other exceptional women, has spurred me on to finally finish this book.

The world is a much better place with us in it, but women all over the world are living in their boxes, isolated and alone, putting on brave faces and accepting their lot.

We need to be honest about how we are feeling, how valuable we are and why we are not achieving our potential.

Think about Britney Spears. She is at the top of her industry and has sold over 150 million records but has been legally enslaved for 13 years, in the so called "free world".

If slavery of women can happen in the public gaze, then what about the rest of us women, behind closed doors?

Without women, humankind would die out and that is a fact.

As individuals we may feel powerless, but we can use our voices in private and in public, we can write words to be published and contact those in power.

As a group we can be more vocal, write more emails, books, articles, start campaigns and put pressure on our managers and Government.

As a large group we can be inspired, energised and empowered. We can do anything but we can't do everything unless we allocate tasks around the home to free up our time so that we can make changes.

You might not be liked for it at first, but you will be respected for it and over time you will get what you want.

But first you need space and time to think. You need to decide what you want and you need to ask for it.

As far as I know, people can't read our minds so gather help if you need it.

We need to keep asking and keep getting. After all, if you don't ask for what you want, how are you going to get it?

Imagine what we could do if we put our hearts, brains and bodies into improving the world for women and families, instead of wasting energy collecting crumbs and wiping worktops.

How to use this book

In this book, I have channelled the famous quote by Emmeline Pankhurst, "Deeds not words" and used the modern mantra of "Words and actions".

Therefore, throughout the book I have included some exercises:

- **Ideas to Action** – this will get you thinking by asking yourself some questions.

- **Actions to Empower** – you can then use these actions to reconnect with your true self and to help you reach your true potential.

Look at the world today. There are wars across the globe killing innocent babies, ruination of the planet by greed and carelessness and half the population, the women who gave us life, are being seconded to a double life of drudgery and a half life of meaning.

And we are allowing this to happen by staying silent and not being active in the exterior world. I've had enough of it. Have you?

We need to recognise that WE HAVE THE POWER to create change.

So, take off the heavy weight of your 'womanhood', look around you, let's take control and let's take action!

CHAPTER 1

My Why

I WAS ASKED THE question, "What qualifies you to write a book on this subject?" My answer is that I have over 50 years of lived experience as a woman, I have read feminist literature over decades, I have female children and have many female friends, relatives and acquaintances, with similar experiences to me, despite having so much talent, insight, wit and wisdom.

By giving you the details of my own experience, I hope that you too will critique your own personal experiences of being a woman and possibly being a mother and see that behind closed doors, you and women up and down the country and across the globe, are all working hard, mentally, physically and emotionally and literally going around in circles, not daring to dream, never mind fulfilling your potential.

I've backed this up with research from Maslow to Mumsnet, so you have the information at hand for you, your friends and your daughters.

I was a very different girl before I got married and had kids. I would dance until the early hours, run like the wind, play football with the boys and skip the washing up.

Having gone to school on a housing estate, a few of us kids were given extra lessons to pass the 11+ exam to go to a grammar school. More girls than boys were in the top sets and I passed and went to an outstanding grammar school, Upton Hall Convent FCJ.

I got a great education and did well in my GCSEs but decided to do a secretarial course like my friends. Would a boy have decided to do this, would his teachers have thought it was a good idea without trying to talk him out of it?

When I got my first job as a secretary, I realised with a sinking heart that I had made a big mistake. My peers presumed I was dumb which enraged me so I decided to go to night school to do an A-Level in my favourite subject, English Literature. I understood then that I would have to go to university to get a career job.

Needing money for further education, I switched to another low expectation job (but better salary) in order to save up. My boss heard about my aspiration to go to university and threatened that if I didn't agree to stay at

the company, he would "throw me in the typing pool".
He said some people like his son had brains and I didn't.
I doubt he even spent the time to look at my CV.

Luckily for me (I like to think of the positive), I had a
car crash, got whiplash and while I recuperated, used the
brain I was told I didn't have, saved the insurance
money and went to the University of Glamorgan, thanks
to a great guy called Rob Middlehurst, who was the
Professor handling admissions.

After stretching my intellectual brain, living
independently, learning about myself and others from
all over the country, it was time to leave. I had mixed
with academically gifted people who I had held in awe
beforehand – spoiler, they are just the same as you and
me, but great at writing essays!

When I graduated and was thinking about my career,
London, where all the jobs were at the time, was way out
of my comfort zone. I was a girl from a small Northern
town after all.

Unfortunately, in 1995 there were few graduate jobs, so
I went back to being a secretary in the local biscuit
factory. Within a week, I realised that in this job I would
be making tea and photocopying for the next 50 years.

I was a self-starter postgraduate, I had good
qualifications. I looked at my first pay packet and
sighed.

However, I used my meagre wage to save a deposit for my very own flat. I was so excited that I nearly drove around the roundabout the wrong way. I had done it on my own!

After about six months, a lovely lad with blue tinted glasses started in his administration job too. He had an outgoing, confident persona and everyone liked him.

My male peer was soon promoted as a 'natural progression'. I wasn't identified as having talents or skills. despite having an honours degree in communication studies which could have been adapted to any role.

Yet I was stuck behind a desk, taking shorthand and making the boss coffee at 10.30am and tea at 3pm. (Yes, this still happened in 1997!). If I didn't do this on time, he would get very annoyed. I had to get out of this culture and away from this misogynistic boss. It really was 'jobs for the boys'.

Not long after, there was an opportunity from head office to get some bright ideas to increase profits and processes. I volunteered for it. From there I went on to take on another project for Red Nose Day, with the aim of raising money for this fabulous charity by holding a number of events with staff.

The lady whose idea it was to do a Women's Institute style nude calendar (like the Calendar Girls' film) said she didn't have time to do it. I suspected her bullying husband put a stop to it, but that's another story.

She told me to develop it and I did. I did the makeup for all the beautiful young girls and the not so beautiful old men and photographed them in an array of fancy-dress outfits which were kindly donated from the local shop.

Once the make-up was on, I photographed them, in various fun poses and chose the best ones to make into a calendar.

As a thank you, we were invited to go to London to watch the BBC live event with two of my heroes, Graham Norton and Vanessa Feltz. I couldn't help thinking that the colleague who started off the project should have been there with me.

By then, time was ticking on and after a concerned call from my godmother about how I would be left on the shelf (at 28) I got a reality check that 'I couldn't have fun forever'.

Soon after that I was lucky enough to meet my partner for life. He nudged me to go for another job and that's when I finally got on the career ladder.

I worked hard at it, day, night and weekends, studying marketing to get more skills and qualifications and began five years of progression. I was motivated and satisfied, learning new skills and taking on more responsibility. It was the most rewarding role I had done since studying at university and I was promoted.

Unfortunately, after 5 happy years, the company was bought out and the new company didn't value the past work of employees and definitely didn't see the value in a pregnant woman managing events for them, so in 2008, coinciding with the global financial crisis, I was made redundant from my much-loved job and spent all the money at Mamas and Papas.

So here ended the years of hard work, long days, dedication, knowledge, skills, experience, qualifications, colleagues, networks and even baby gifts. I was no longer an asset.

Stuck at home alone, out of a career girl's comfort zone, with hormones running riot, worries about the labour, the pain of labour itself, a new baby, painful stitches, sleepless nights, changes in my body and breastfeeding, I learnt that a female is dropped from the workforce when she is at her weakest and needing the most support. Did this happen to you?

Chances are that many companies lose their most loyal, skilled and hard-working employees in this way. It is a poor choice financially for maintaining their most experienced workforce. It's called a skills 'leak' and companies allow this during women's lifetimes as they lose their female staff after pregnancy, during peri-menopause and menopause, or any other female-related issues.

Years later, having gone to a Parent Preneur network group, I mentioned my story to a group of six parents, three had experienced exactly the same treatment from their middle management corporate jobs. It doesn't have to be like this.

Forward thinking companies should be supporting half the population in their transition into parenthood. They could have on-site crèches (and earn money too) while the parents are supported. This would ensure that the employees' valuable knowledge, skills and experience remain in the company.

On maternity leave, I decided I needed to push forward and set up an online magazine for women called Futurepink.com with a grant from UnLtd, a social entrepreneur's charity, based in Leeds.

I gathered women columnists to write about real life skills such as 'How to Manage Money', 'How to Fix Your Car' and even had an Agony Aunt. I had a team of 10 women who came to meetings and wrote regularly. We even promoted the brand by wearing fuchsia pink at Aintree Ladies Day and got in the national press.

Ironically, as the magazine was beginning to get traction with 33,000 views and sponsored by Wirralbiz and others, I became pregnant again and was working long hours into the night to get the copy published. Something had to give and I decided I couldn't move house, have a new baby and run a magazine.

Having read a lot of Mumsnet posts, I know that many, many women go through similar experiences and I want you to know that the subsequent loss of your identity is real, it is challenging and you are not alone.

Do you have female friends and relatives who had a bright future ahead of them but were thwarted in their hopes and dreams? This happens every day to half the population.

Then those same women spend hours performing meaningless, repetitive tasks like wiping worktops, chopping cheese, cleaning, tidying, organising and re-organising.

When I tried to get back into work with 2 young children and a husband who worked very long hours, I got a job in a manufacturing company who said they were flexible to family life.

However, in reality this 'flexibility' stretched to leaving work half an hour early once a week. This helped me avoid the traffic somewhat, but I still had to drive an hour back to the children should an emergency happen. This left me stressed and with a very fast heartbeat as I was hyper aware that in the day, I had sole responsibility to get to the children should they have an accident.

The next temporary job I took was in the charity sector which offered low pay in an administrative role (despite it having management tasks). With little support and a large workload that didn't allow for a lunch break, I managed to fit it in between school hours so I could drop off and collect my children on time.

The third was in a dentist with part-time hours, but with the expectation of achieving full time results, including managing the social media until late in the evening, but without payment of those hours.

So, despite my qualifications, experience and formerly brilliant career record, I was 'let go' from these jobs and I experienced the shame and frustration of not being able to contribute to the exterior world.

The shame should be on the companies who 'let down' the unique contribution that Mothers provide in the workplace and shame on them for inadequate management.

In hindsight, I now realise that I was set up for failure and my contributions were diminished, demeaned and undervalued.

I suspect I am not alone in my private, painful experiences. If you know any women who have been "let go of" the truth is often that they have been let down. What is your story?

How do any of these roles adapt to, or support family life? Yet more than half of the population are being penalised for taking the supporting role. Again, women are undermined and unsupported. Women, being women, often blame themselves for the shortcomings of their employers. Did something similar happen to you?

When 'something has to give' it is the woman who does the giving, supporting the economy and enabling the next generation to get a good education, a good group of friends, confidence-building hobbies and has the huge responsibility of moulding the next generation of humans.

But for this there is low status, no pay, little reward and few perks. It is the woman who pays again. She loses her independence, her identity, her salary, her career, her perks and her peers. Would you apply for this position?

If she returns to work, she will work hard all day and return to a full-time second job of responsibility for her household and all those who live in it.

Why are women doing this in their droves?

We all need to communicate, speak up and write down our individual experiences, to draw attention to these injustices, create change and make our hopes and dreams possible for ourselves and our children.

My hope in writing this book is that we can all recognise that the society we live in systematically limits, diverts, dismisses, diminishes, demeans, enslaves and undermines women.

We need to change this and unlock the huge intellectual potential of 51% of the population.

If you owned a company, would you put your brightest, most skilled and determined employees to work wiping worktops?

No, neither would I. But hey, that's the way it is in society today.

This is a huge block in society's progression and it has to stop!

What I've learned is that no matter what these external forces tell you to be and do, your true self is still there, dormant, waiting for you to lift your head up again.

When I had the idea to write a book (honestly it's been inside my mind since 1994) I was so frustrated for myself and for all the women I read about and knew and loved.

I didn't know how to start, I didn't think I could do it and I doubted my ability to complete it, but I made it my mission as I was so frustrated for all the talented women I met.

It has been a huge personal journey and as I started to believe I could do it, I invested in myself and got the tools to enable me; coloured pens, paper, sticky notes, tabs, highlighters, folders and a life coach (thanks Beth Penfold) to break down some of the barriers and negative beliefs that had been built up in my mind, by living in this society.

I started to reconnect to my individual dreams, desires and purpose.

I am now ready to take off the hood that has weighed heavily on me and you may not know it yet, but you too have been #Womanhooded.

In the next chapter I will tell you more, so that we can reach our potential together.

CHAPTER 2

Herstory

IN THIS CHAPTER I'M going to look at how females are socialised to behave in certain ways.

In 2023, in one of the world's most successful and progressive companies in the world, Apple, their software dictionary, Catalina OS Version 10.15.7, flags up the word 'herstory' as a mistake, not even recognising it as a word. I say this not to directly criticise Apple, who is also responsible for designing the format and providing me with the software to write this book. However, it flags up that this is a direct reflection of society at this moment in time.

The word 'history' is supposed to represent the whole of humankind, but does it? Is half the planet still being hidden and hooded? History is what we learn in our school's curriculum, on TV, in books, in magazines, in billions of references online, in the media, on social media, in photographs, in classical paintings and in statues.

You may think that your thoughts and feelings are unique and that you are isolated and alone but please be assured that you are not. Women have been struggling to gain respect, equality and to forge their own identities for centuries. It is highly personal to you and it is highly political for us all.

Although the origin of the phrase 'the personal is political' is uncertain, it was popular after the publication in 1970 of an essay of the same name by American feminist Carol Hanisch. She argued that many of our personal experiences (particularly those of women) can be traced to our situation within a system of powerful and powerless relationships.

Hanisch's essay focused on men's power and women's oppression. For example, if a particular woman is being abused by a male partner, then societal acceptance of the treatment of women is an important factor in explaining this abuse.

She wasn't the first to suggest that personal experiences are the result of a social structure or inequality. In 1959 an American sociologist, C Wright Mills published 'The Sociological Imagination'. In this he argued that individual experiences are inextricably connected with the greater social and historical experience. For example, if an individual is unemployed, then it may be related to larger patterns of unemployment in society at the time.

The context of our experience is important in the social sciences. In 'The Feminine Mystique' (1963), American author and feminist, Betty Friedan referred to "the problem that has no name" in which women felt constrained, unsatisfied and unhappy in their roles as wives, mothers and homemakers, despite being outwardly perceived as a success in society.

This dissatisfaction was often treated as an individual problem, both by their doctors and the women themselves, Friedan took the helicopter view, as all these women shared common experiences, then she extrapolated the facts and saw the link to the role of women in society.

The Feminine Mystique was criticised as only specific to white middle-class women, but her book came to be considered crucial in feminist history and theory. Friedan's arguments were highly influential for second wave feminism in the 1960s and 1970s.

Women's discussion groups were called 'therapy' which suggested a fault in them. However, she believed that women's personal problems were political problems, because they were caused by women's inequality. Consequently, these problems could not be solved by individual solutions alone, but by social change.

At the beginning of the twenty-first century, 'the personal is political' was key to understanding various feminist issues that might otherwise have been seen as purely 'personal'. For example, the association of being thin with a woman's perceived success.

American feminist scholar and activist Bell Hooks stressed the origins of feminist theory in women's personal experiences. She discussed her own childhood experiences as a young black girl, in which she felt constrained in her family by gender ideologies. Because Hooks could not identify or communicate with her family regarding this, she sought to better understand her condition. Theory and politics were intimately connected to her personal life.

We all have individual stories to tell, which are being gathered by the UK government post lockdown, which is heartening. If you were writing YOUR experience of lockdown, it would most certainly differ from the experience of a white, middle class male columnist of a national newspaper.

Yet, these past versions of events have been written and recorded and presented as the 'truth' of our collective experience, rather than simply one carefully crafted and edited version of one point of view.

The American sociologist Patricia Hill Collins in her book 'Black Feminist Thought: Knowledge, Consciousness, and the Politics of Empowerment'

(1990)[1] proposed a standpoint theory that emphasized black women's oppression - a system whereby race, gender and class oppression gives African American women a distinct point of view due to their marginalized status.

She demonstrated how African American women are oppressed by economic labour exploitation, denial of their rights and subject to controlling cultural images that create damaging stereotypes[2].

Hill Collins suggested that African American women can give a unique perspective to feminist scholarship so asked for it to be more inclusive[3] and reject knowledge that dehumanizes and objectifies people.

If you look back in history, you can imagine how this same system of writing and editing events and experiences has been continuing letter by letter for seconds, minutes, hours, days, weeks, months, years, decades and centuries, over the passage of time.

Winston Churchill himself even said it in his famous quote "History will be kind to me for I intend to write it."

---

[1] https://www.britannica.com/biography/Patricia-Hill-Collins
[2] https://www.merriam-webster.com/dictionary/stereotypes
[3] https://www.merriam-webster.com/dictionary/inclusive

The Arts

Women have long been written out of *HIStory* and thankfully this is now being noticed and addressed by museums and historical institutions as an increasing number of female statues are being commissioned. A simple count of the statues in London has shown how disproportionate statues of celebrated men contrast with the number of celebrated women.

In the political, social, arts and everyday world, women in history are being revisited and oversights and omissions are being corrected so that a gender balanced legacy can be seen.

It has taken until 2018 for a statue of Emmeline Pankhurst, the leader of the suffragette movement and one of the most iconic women's rights activists in British history, to be unveiled in her home city of Manchester. This is years after she fought for British women to be given the vote in a General Election. It took 100 years, but it is there now.

The phrase 'see it, be it' is being used now as girls must first see a role model, to be a role model for the next generation.

You too can use your skills and talents in photography, poetry, drawing or painting to prove your existence. Put your full name clearly and in large letters where it can be seen, so that other women and men looking at your work can see that a woman has produced the piece. It encourages other women to do the same and one by one our abilities will be seen and celebrated more.

The Written Word

Women in the 1800s routinely used men's names so that they could be printed or taken seriously as authors and even J K Rowling used letters to be ambiguous when she began her career.

To prove your existence and leave a legacy, write an email, a letter, an essay, a column or a book. Make sure you put your full name and any qualifications with it, to add weight to whatever you write.

Once you have started to write and get into the habit of noticing and changing things around you, it will get easier and this will give you more confidence in other areas of your life.

Make it known that a woman had that idea, made that difference or told that story in a magazine article. By taking an active step, you are also encouraging other women to do the same and make writing the 'norm' for more women.

Jane Austen was unusual in that she wrote under her full name for her novels, but initially started out by calling herself 'a lady'. Perhaps it was the subject matter of marriage and romance that allowed her to be acknowledged in this arena, the interior world of a 'woman's domain'.

Appreciation of her major published works is still strong today as many are on the GCSE and A-Level curriculum for English literature in the UK education system.

Despite her short writing career, she remains one of the most well-known and admired writers in British literary history.

However, it begs the question, how many other novelists who wrote about the exterior world were thwarted simply because they were women?

You could put aside 20 minutes a day to start developing your writing skills and proving your place as a woman in history and leave a legacy for people to read and look at for generations to come.

The evidence is clear about the poor treatment and representation of some humans, ie women. It's there in the written word, in photographs, on screen and on everyone's mobile phones for all to see.

We still have a long way to go in 2024 in the genre of video, because if you watch music videos today, it seems like the world has not moved on for women.

In fact, it's worse, because we are enlightened but we are still ignoring the power imbalance and the same old tired messages are being churned out.

'Sex sells' has been an advertising excuse for even presenting scantily clad women on cars. This really means women's sexiness sells to MEN, so women have been routinely harnessed and used to sell products and services from peanuts to pop music.

Don't get me wrong, I adore Duran Duran, but in their iconic pop video, Rio in 1983, a beautiful, slim, painted woman cavorts on a boat in a tiny swimming costume, while the males look at her and chase her. They are mostly fully clothed wearing suits. I know the story of this is that they lost their luggage, so only had the suits they travelled in to wear, but what excuse have all the other videos got?

Another video, 20 years later in 2004 by the talented R&B singer and dancer Christina Milian, shows us the same old formula in her most successful single to date called 'Dip it Low'. The line 'dip it low' and the sweet tone of her voice stick in your mind, perpetuating the stereotype of women as a sexual plaything. Have we really dipped this low?

Where is the nubile, naive and wide-eyed young male bending over backwards and forwards for our entertainment? To be honest, I don't want to see it.

Another 10 years later in dance music videos, the sexually provocative moves of female singers as they perform for the viewer is uncomfortable. I've not paid for a dance in a lap dancing club, I've not made the effort to plan my night, catch a cab, meet up with a friend, queue for an hour, buy an entry ticket, buy an overpriced drink or actively buy a dance. I've simply pressed a random button on a remote-control device and been given an insight into a seedy world of power-play, where youth and beauty are used by a director and writer, to coerce an inexperienced young woman to writhe around in her underwear. How demeaning is that?

In 2024, the message is clear - talented and successful women are still normalised as ornaments to be looked at and judged, semi-naked. This seems old-fashioned and boring now, yet it still goes on.

What stays in my mind whilst I am channel hopping to music videos today, is how little the women seem to wear and how misogynistic and pervasive these videos are in the guise of entertaining us.

How about a young woman flying a plane, driving a car, doing some kick ass moves or modelling being a CEO of a company? Surely that's more in tune with the present. It's a new, fresh and more interesting perspective. Do you agree?

One recent revelation and inspiration has been that a feminist film made by a team of women has attracted a huge audience and made £1.1 billion. The concept of a Barbie movie which led to the casting, acting, production, direction, re-branding and marketing of an updated Barbie has proven to be the biggest box office success of 2023 according to Ian Youngs, Arts and Entertainment Reporter of BBC online (4 Sept 2023).

Let's hope it leads the way for many more in the future.

Think as I might, I can't think of one video where a young male writhes around like his life depends on it, to lure another human. Can you? If so, please message me on instagram at @iamjoannalambe.

How did we get here?

Firstly, females are nurtured very differently from males at a very early age, with a colour signal to the world that they are female, by being dressed in pale pink baby grows, with pink blankets and pink accessories and then later their girl status further extends to pink frilly tutus, pink dresses and even pink shoes!

Female babies are often described as 'pretty' and male babies as 'big' often reinforced by passersby as they stop to look in a pram. Therefore, from a very young age and in the wider community, expectations, reinforcement and identity of a female baby on her attractiveness is often the focus of the conversation.

I have also been a part of this socialisation process. Having rejoiced in the fact that I was having a baby girl, I went around all the shops and "oohed and ahhed" about the softest materials in the latest colours and designs, mostly pale pink.

Later as my baby girl grew into a toddler, I rejoiced in buying other pink clothes from ski suits to skirts, in varying shades of pink from coral to fuchsia!

My first born conformed to her pink world and happily wore her frilly dresses and pink tights. At the same time, her friends were happily wearing their pink outfits too and going around nursery acting like girls 'should'. I often received reports from nursery assistants to say that she was a 'good girl' and had behaved really well. However, in hindsight what does that even mean? Basically, she had not given the staff any trouble, she had done what she was told to do and when she was told to do it.

When my second daughter was born, I had saved all the clothes from my first child and had been given on top of that a huge black plastic bin bag of pink clothes (thanks Lulu) as well as a huge amount of new pink clothes by family and friends.

Therefore, a female child is socialised to fit into their peer group and society yet again.

It strikes me that we notice dress codes immediately. However, there are hundreds of thousands of 'norming' behaviours that a child and a mother are acting out, gaining feedback on and re-enacting every day, which are more subtle.

Have you ever seen or heard of a male baby being dressed in pink? What would you think if you did? What would you say to the parents? In our society, I think the mother would be seen as questionable if they dressed a child in pink.

I wonder what would have happened if I put my girl child in a blue playsuit and what my peers would have said or thought about me?

In turn, I too was socialised.

When I was a young girl of around 10 years old (in the 1980s) my cousins and I were bought Girls World dolls which were life size dolls heads (sounds weird today) with shoulder length hair and a middle piece of hair that could be extended to make it longer than the rest. It came with a selection of makeup including red and pink lipstick, blue eyeshadow and fake eyelashes.

My nan must have seen an advert for it and decided that it was a good present for young girls. I looked it up recently on YouTube and it was described as "especially for girls to learn about makeup and hairstyling" with the background message "it's a different world for a growing up girl." It seems times haven't changed much, 40 years later.

The ad for Girls World appeared in a joint ad with a product called Kitchen Centre "two great growing up ideas for girls." Thus, teaching us girls what is expected of us and how to act. Imagine if this appeared as an ad called Boys World?

Most girls are still learning how to act in society and women are still responsible for the home, in the interior world, but on top of this they are also expected to manage the outside (exterior world of work). This is a huge burden for women.

In the next chapter, I'm going to look at other role models we have learned about from a young age and who we still aspire to today.

Ideas to Action

1. Think about what you liked wearing as a child?

2. What are the females in your favourite music videos wearing?

3. What are the females in your favourite music videos doing?

4. What are the males in the videos wearing?

5. What are the males in the videos doing?

6. What would you like to see women wearing in music videos?

7. What would be new and interesting to see women do in music videos?

8. What would you like to see more of?

9. What would you like to see less of?

10. What is the best example of female role modelling in videos?

Actions to Empower

1. Post your thoughts on social media to see what reactions you get such as
I saw ....(doing or wearing)
in their video. I thought it was very boring/old fashioned/overtly sexual.
What's wrong about portraying women like this, time and time again?

2. Follow, tag or message me on Instagram @iamjoannalambe

3. Follow and engage with those artists who don't copy the same old
patriarchal formula.

4. What do you wear to go out at the weekend?
Change your look if necessary to what is more practical, stylish and suits your
lifestyle. Are your feet hurting at the end of the night? If they do, buy different
ones that don't hurt.

5. What outfit do you wear to work or the office?
Change your look so it is practical for the role you want to have.

6. What do you wear on your days off? Is it practical, individual or fun?
If not, change it.

7. What does wearing these outfits prevent you from doing, such as
running, dancing?

8. Do these outfits help you do certain things? If so repeat, if not change them.

9. Give yourself positive self-talk, such as "I am so comfortable in these
superb new shoes."

10. Pat yourself on the arm as you say it out loud, to reinforce your behaviour,
so you do it more and more.

CHAPTER 3

Cinderella and Other Role Models

IN THIS CHAPTER I aim to further show how you are socialised into a 'female ideal' and how to rethink it to be more 'yourself'.

Right from their very birth, girls are set on the path of learning how 'to be feminine'. How to look, what to wear, what to eat or not to eat, how to behave and how to wear their hair (preferably long and blonde), how to aspire to glossy rosebud lips, to get the 'wide-eyed look' (of a naive child) by coating their eyelashes and using makeup to look beautiful to attract a mate.

By the time you enter womanhood, you have been effectively and systematically 'groomed' to look pretty, to enable and support, to serve and to soothe.

Hopefully by the end of this book, you can take off your *hood* and view the world above. I hope too that you can achieve a more balanced and fulfilled role in society and reach your full potential as a human being.

As a 21 year old woman looking for direction in life, I bought a fantastic book called 'The Cinderella Complex' in Disney World. The irony was not lost on me as I entered a perfectly constructed land of fun, smiles and laughter, when the reality for the workers was that they had a lot of menial work to do, sweeping up litter, frying the millionth French fry, all with a smile on their faces to live up to the Disney image and "whistle while they worked".

It may be a fairy tale, but as one of the first stories women have ever been told, it is easy to see how we have been socialised to believe in the dream of 'if you are beautiful and a good girl, you will escape your hard, cruel, loveless, menial life and be saved by a handsome prince'. The same old story has been drilled into us via the genre of film, with modern day re-telling of the same messages via romantic stories such as An Officer and a Gentleman, Pretty Woman and countless more.

When women today get married, or live with their partners, the vast majority swap a band of gold for a lifetime of servitude, to their partners, to their children (if and when they have them) and to their wider family.

One morning I even went downstairs to find a mountain of Rice Krispies where my daughter had tried to get her own favourite breakfast cereal and failed, which meant that I had to pick individual Rice Krispies off the floor (Cinderella picked up individual lentils). The re-enactment of the story was not lost on me as I fell to the floor to clean it up.

With 18 years of servitude, (when the first child reaches adulthood and then add extra years for each subsequent child) this timeline ensures that most women's productive lives are concentrated on the mundane drudgery of cooking, cleaning, caring, meal preparations, shopping, hoovering, tidying, mopping up, wiping bottoms, floors, doors, toilets, planning, organising, re-organising, chauffeuring, in a daily pattern of eat, sleep and repeat.

Therefore, the truth of marriage and motherhood is often the opposite of these tales, as women struggle to juggle their home, children and jobs to live up to this 'perfect' image.

If you think about it, it is not much different from the experience of Cinderella BEFORE she met the prince, not AFTER. Cleaning the floor, making dinner, brushing hair and sewing dresses, to enable other people in the house to live their best lives.

Putting herself at the bottom of 'the list', feeling lowly, being lonely, losing her identity (as a princess), her independence and possibly losing her mind, she is in the situation of having no money and nowhere else to go. Sound familiar?

Added to all this, a woman also has the pressure to look great in order to attract a mate. This is the sub-text of the story, that girls like Cinderella must be beautiful, kind and passive to their oppressors and be sweet to escape their dreary life. And as if she hasn't got enough to do in her life, she must wear pretty, uncomfortable shoes!

In contrast, messages from films such as Disney's heroes, which are generally men, are that they actively *'vanquish'*, *'conquer'* and lift their romantic interest off their feet.

What if they don't want to be lifted up by an overpowering, entitled narcissist?

This was the only option available to a poor girl - marry into money and status - because she surely couldn't make enough money on her own!

Witches

Some women have been viewed with suspicion as far back as the 1400s.

If a woman was single or old, independent or had a cat for company, she would have been viewed with suspicion and assumed to be a witch, especially if she had the misfortune of having a mole.

As for wearing a hooded cloak, it probably meant she was cold, or shy, or didn't want to attract attention as a single female.

She may simply have been making herbal remedies for calm and tranquility, or for the good of someone's health. She may have been a menopausal woman treating her ailments.

Or perhaps a grieving widow, who lived longer than her spouse and was searching for answers or remedies for their grief.

In the 1700s witches were put on trial for their supposed crimes. They were drowned, hanged or burned, if they didn't confess to their crimes. They were sentenced to death either way.

Were they a threat to society or were they sought out in return for a month's salary? Were they outspoken? Were they a threat to the social order where the male offered sanctuary from the outside world (in return for sex?).

By being an independent woman, the men folk may have felt threatened, so they felt the need to send a message to other females, that women living on their own would be shunned and possibly murdered.

I wonder what skills, knowledge and remedies we lost from this culling?

Universities in history departments across the country are now researching and revisiting the role of witches in society and how and why they were viewed with fear and disdain and ultimately why they were sentenced to death.

As we know, our ears and nose continue growing all our life, which is where the stereotype of a witch with a mole and a large nose comes from. Were they really nasty and evil or were they feared for being independent? Were they simply powerless and poor, so easily disposed. Were they murdered for their house or land? They were at the very least misunderstood.

So even from the time girls can read (and even younger when they are read to) they are being taught about women and their roles in society and in their own home. This is bad enough, but when most people in the twenty-first century can't live on one income anymore, they then have to work inside AND outside the home.

As for the boys in society, it is not fair on them either, as they struggle too. They are repressed in many ways, to conform to being a 'man', they feel they can't talk to their friends about their feelings or their worries without appearing 'weak'. They are expected to absorb stress and repress their emotions or they will look 'less masculine'.

And for a woman, the message is reinforced again and again, if you wish to find a handsome prince, who is going to 'save' you, then you need to fit into the Cinderella mould, as below:

Be blonde – like the most desirable women of the times; Barbie, Britney, Cinderella, Madonna, Marilyn Monroe and Pamela Anderson.

Despite having dark hair, you too might bleach your hair or go to the hairdressers to have it lightened, lifted, have a balayage, highlighted etc. Why is this?

Is it because *YOU* like blonde hair or is it because you have been socialised to believe that blonde hair is more beautiful and 'blondes have more fun'?

Is it also the Hollywood guide to being feminine, sexually attractive and available to men, as per Marilyn Monroe who was naturally a redhead but made into a 'blonde bombshell'.

Be thin - Cinderella was likely underfed as she was physically neglected and enslaved. She was malnourished and didn't grow properly. (That's likely why her feet were so small that no-one else could fit into them)!

The diet industry today is a *multi-million-pound* industry built to aid being slim. It's embedded in western culture that thin equals *'beautiful'*.

In the rest of the developing world, being thin means starving or underfed.

Thank goodness we went from Kate Moss to Kim Kardashian's body shape in my lifetime. A lot of women breathed a huge sigh of relief that day, as the new curvy, more womanly shape was celebrated. Whatever you think of Kim, she started a new trend where women could eat without feeling guilty or purging themselves.

Be subservient - Cinderella was at the beck and call of her step-mother and step-sisters. If they needed a dress fixed, she did it, if they needed their hair putting up, she did it. This is presented as the pinnacle of what a 'good girl' does.

You are also taught to be a 'good girl', whatever that is, not to 'make a fuss' even if you are wronged and generally to support and enable your male counterparts.

Think about this:-

- Who gets the kettle on in your home?
- Who provides the cake?
- Who prepares the room for guests?
- Who decides the menu?
- Who organises the family schedule?
- Who plans how to entertain any guests?

Girls and boys look at their own parents as role models. We've all sat at a table where someone plays 'mum' and puts the tea in our cups, or the water in our glass, despite the whole family being there. If you see this behaviour many times, it is easy to see how entrenched and expected it becomes.

Obey – we are told Cinderella had a sweet nature and was loyal to her step-family and despite their treatment she gave them a home, depending on which version you read. The story of Britney Spears' conservatorship and enslavement is not so different today.

Be beautiful – this is a multi-billion-pound industry. Pressure from adverts alone ensure that girls and women have a similar model fed into their brain every minute of every day whatever TV show they consume, or social media, magazine, newspaper, TV programme, clothing or makeup site.

However, this narrow spectrum is now expanding to reflect other ideas of beauty including different types of skin and different ages, as current trends focus more on health.

It is fine to want to improve yourself, but spending so much time on reapplying makeup, injecting lips to look like blow up sex dolls and putting filters on every picture seems unhealthy.

It is your body, so you can choose to do what you want with it, to improve your confidence and self-worth however, we need a balance of improving our mind as well as our bodies. We are not purely ornaments, but complex human beings.

You are constantly bombarded with 'messages' from TV, films, radio, music, videos, YouTube, Netflix, Facebook, Instagram, friends, family and role models, that you consciously and unconsciously absorb. This is how you view yourself and what you compare yourself to, to try and conform and learn what's acceptable for a female and what's unacceptable for a female.

This is why role models and influencers are so important. They open the door for what is acceptable, what is normal and can start a conversation about any topics that are close to their heart. They can influence their fans and audience and are in a really powerful position, hence why advertisers seek them out, as they can literally make or break a product or service.

The majority of TV you watch is decided for you by unknown teams with their own agenda, which is mostly to increase their audience and attract the most money in sponsorship. This doesn't help you, as it is a formula for shows that have been tried and tested and therefore it is in the interests of channels to produce low budget shows that appeal to the masses such as Love Island and I'm a Celebrity, Get Me Out of Here.

You may think it is mindless TV, but you and your family are taking in powerful messages whether you like it or not.

Therefore, you need to carefully choose what you consume from brochures, catalogues, TV shows, films, books and magazines, where you are being constantly harassed by adverts to buy their products. Even if you glance at them, your eyes absorb the messages.

Remember the famous song which preached "do not read beauty magazines, they will only make you feel ugly" by Baz Luhurman? How true is this statement for you? Do magazines still show you perfect images that 99% of us can only dream of reaching. The famous model, Cindy Crawford, with sharp insight once said, "Not even I wake up looking like Cindy Crawford!"

Successful women's magazines produce copy to appeal to the masses and sell stuff. To do that, ads have to create a need, a flaw or a problem, which they solve with their 'miracle solution' be it a spot cream, hair spray or diet product - the list is endless. What if putting on a couple of pounds was not a problem? Then the diet product wouldn't be bought and women would be happier, but companies would not be richer because the product wouldn't be bought.

Ironically, if we had more fat on our bodies, we would probably survive some situations such as a famine or freezing weather conditions, as we would be warmer and have more fat stores to use up until we found food.

Here lies the problem.

Capitalism and contentment are opposite sides of a coin. You are presented as 'unhappy', 'flawed' or 'imperfect' before you buy a product and as this message is being shouted at you a thousand times a day, how can you ignore it?

We all put weight on over winter, it's natural to all animals and keeps us warm and alive. It's a throwback from when food wasn't as abundant in cave times.

Yet women up and down the country are still feeling guilty for eating chocolate, cakes or desserts and putting on weight.

What if you used more of your energy and attention to focus on your dreams, talents and skills?
Women are judged by their peers, themselves, their partners, their employers, their staff, their audience, their community, their company, their acquaintances, their friends, their children, their children's friends, parents and society, on what they wear and what weight they are. Not on what they say or do.

In my opinion, women spend too much time and effort thinking and talking about what they should wear, or their hair style, or what bag to buy. It is sometimes fun and how capitalism thrives, but surely we have deeper needs than the surface that we must address too?

In contrast, spending so much energy on what we look like or want to look like, is not what the male population does. Being a male means in general that they spend time learning new skills, focusing on the outside world, reading about their hobbies, finance, investments and law, progressing their careers, reaching their potential and making informed decisions on what they've read.

However, it was predicted by Naomi Wolf in The Beauty Myth (1990) that one day men would similarly spend time on these endeavours. Unfortunately, she was right, as you now see a lot of younger men with tattoos, sculpted beards, strict skin care regimes, man bags and obsessing over their gym bodies.

I'd like to think that the real me is not judged on what I wear or what I weigh, but on what I have to say, how I treat others, what I contribute to society, how I raise my children and how I make other people FEEL because ultimately that is what other people remember.
It constantly surprises me that a woman will look at herself and see her *flaws*, be self-deprecating to compliments and generally keep herself down.

What is your response to a compliment? Is it self-deprecating, like "What, this old thing?" The chances are that you responded something like this, as we have been conditioned to not get 'too big for our boots'. Did you feel embarrassed? Why?

Guess what ladies - you need to accept the compliment. You simply need to say, "thank you" and smile. If you want to elevate it even more, you could return the compliment and pass on the positivity.

We all have a strong social urge to be accepted and from school age, it has been shown that girls look to other girls and boys for affirmation and continue to do so, the cliché "does my bum look big in this?" is there for a reason.

In our capitalist society, success is measured in terms of riches, not how funny you are (unless you become a comedian), how kind you are or how emotionally intelligent you are (unless you get the right kind of high-paying job).

Are you a nurturing team player, which is one of the key components of feminine styles of leadership? Women at the top of FTSE companies are now recognised for their feminine styles of leadership, which have contributed to their companies' success. They have used these qualities to their advantage. This is in opposition to what the tough masculine style of management used to be and still is.

Women work best in collaborative groups, listening, taking turns to talk and enabling each other. You need to surround yourself with supportive friends to achieve your dreams too.

We need to dig deep and ask ourselves questions and value our OWN opinions.

Have you ever stopped to think how much happier, richer and productive you would be if you put effort into your own individual hopes and dreams and not this pre-set and stringent ideal of being a woman?

If you spent this much time practising the piano you would probably be at Grade 8 or more by now. You may even be an internationally famous pianist.

If you were learning a language, you would be fluent in it and probably two or three more.

If you pursued your own dreams, then you would have reached them by now, instead of going round in circles touching up your roots, trying to reach or maintain your ideal weight, or buying makeup to look even more beautiful. It is never ending.

It's nice to look good and feel confident, but looking beautiful is not an end in itself, it's purely the top layer. Believe me, taking action and achieving your dreams will give you much more confidence and be longer lasting. We can be beautiful and have brains too.

If you continue to make consistent and continued efforts towards your goals, whatever they are, then you can achieve them.

I invite you to dream bigger and take some action.

In the next chapter let's look how girls are socialised to stay small and make way in the exterior world.

Ideas to Action

1. When you were a child what did you dream of becoming?

2. What stopped you?

3. Was it a relative, friend or is it you making excuses?

4. Is there still time to pursue it? If yes, then go for it. If no, can you do it as a hobby?

5. Do you still believe in a fairy tale ending like Cinderella?

6. Do you spend a lot of time going round in circles tidying and cleaning?

7. Do you celebrate your unique self?

8. Do you want to move forwards in your life?

9. Are you the agent in your own life or do you go along with what others want to do?

10. Do you focus too much on what you look like and not what you would like to do instead.

Actions to Empower

① Delegate the following tasks to free up time to do what you want to do: Start with 20 - 60 minutes a day.

Task	Delegate to	So I can
Washing up/filling/emptying dishwasher daily	partner/children	focus and plan my week

② Write a positive storyline for your own life where you are the hero achieving your dreams.

③ Do some research on what you have always wanted to do.

④ Make a phone call and discuss the idea with a supportive friend or family member.

⑤ Plan how you will pursue your dreams in small steps.
I will .... by this date .... tick .....
I will .... by this date .... tick .....
I will .... by this date .... tick .....
I will .... by this date .... tick .....
I will .... by this date .... tick .....

⑥ Get the tools you need, such as folders, books, pens, post-its, highlighters.

⑦ Take the first scary step.

⑧ Take the second scary step.

⑨ Give yourself positive self-talk, such as "I am brilliant at singing."

⑩ Pat yourself on the arm while you say it out loud, for positive reinforcement.

CHAPTER 4

Young Girls and Education

IN THIS CHAPTER WE will look at how girls are pressured inside and outside of school.

Unfortunately, schools are institutions, and the teachers are also institutionalised. They don't plan for the potential sexism in the exterior world, as it's not seen as their job.

Due to the pressures of OFSTED, the goal for teachers these days is to get the most students to pass exams with the best grades. However, surely the role of education is to prepare us for the real world outside?

Don't forget, that young brains are like huge sponges, absorbing all the messages from you and those around you, friends, family, teachers, tutors, TV programmes, films, adverts, radio, women's magazines, newspapers, online news stories, Sunday magazines, books, clothes shops and chemist shops.

Ads are everywhere, espousing taglines such as 'I'm worth it' (*L'Oreal*) but what exactly are you worth? Is your value based on having the most voluminous, coloured hair that is backcombed and kept in place by a strong-smelling hair spray? In these kinds of ads, your value as an attractive female is a given 'truth', the message is to look good for longer with the help of a hairspray.

All of these messages combine, endorse and reinforce ideas of what a female 'should' be to young minds.

In a capitalist society, it doesn't pay for young girls to be happy as they are. It is no wonder that teenage mental health is at a record high, as girls seek approval and affirmation purely on how they look and face immense pressure to conform to current beauty 'ideals'.

Social Media

Added to this, the huge rise in social media and the power of mass influencers (with an audience over 100K), influencers and micro influencers (with an audience of about 10K) enable these female 'role models' to permeate girls' lives with little escape or down time.

Advertising deals with influencers can be lucrative and their female audience is able to replicate a look and purchase any item shown in a couple of clicks.

Many top influencers have used the popularity gained from reality TV programmes which are aimed at young people. Popular contestants are hard to tell apart as they all seem to have huge lashes and lips. The game is to act childlike or naive, in order to gain the sympathy and votes of the viewers. The educated or assertive girls are not popular.

Conversely, reality TV stars turned into influencers are totally unprepared for the added pressures of popularity and fame. They are often unable to process and manage their new life without turning to drink, drugs or unhealthy relationships. They then must live like an animal in a glass box of fame, as the capitalist dream becomes reality.

The painful effects of anonymous audience trolls can exacerbate their distress, often leading to feelings of being imperfect or unworthy, as they compare themselves to their filtered images and their mental health suffers.

As a teenager, I remember looking at many pictures of models in magazines with flawless skin and then comparing them to my own spotty teenage face. Thus began 10 years of drinking lots of water, eating chocolate (as my hormones raged) and then hating myself for my lack of control, then blaming myself for having spots, in a vicious cycle.

It is normal for teenagers to have spots as their hormones settle. It was bad then, but for teenagers now, it is much, much worse and filtered images of perfection are everywhere so that not just faces but reality blurs.

Our girls need balance and escape from this constant bombardment and pressure to conform to generic beauty standards. However, this is a huge global force, as big brands compete for big money.

As an example, my teenage daughter met her friend in Florida one Summer and they turned up in almost identical outfits. The power of global branding was strong, despite them living on different continents.

You may do your hair and makeup and buy the right clothes, but then you have to brush your hair, take the makeup off and get into your pyjamas. Until the next morning, when you repeat the same process again and go round in circles. No wonder we are bored and unsatisfied.

Our girls need to spend less time in virtual reality and more time in real life situations where they can absorb what real people's faces and bodies look like on the beach, in the pool or on the sports field to get a reality check of what is normal.

If each individual, intelligent young girl was receiving messages such as saving, learning and taking action towards their individual hopes and dreams, who knows what they could achieve?

Be Nice

Girls are often told they should be 'nice' or a good girl. But what does that even mean?

To me it means being kind to others, being polite and not pointing out others' physical imperfections or bad points. Also, don't have too strong an opinion and give people more or equal time to talk in a group. Look pretty, be helpful, be thoughtful (of others), dress appropriately, (don't wear too short a skirt, or too low a top) and don't wear too much makeup. Don't take up too much physical space either. What does 'be nice' mean to you?

Being 'good' in school often means listening to the teacher, doing what you are told, not challenging them and being quiet. This makes the job of the teacher much easier, but does it prepare you to cope with life in the world outside?

Next time you are thinking of being 'nice' think about being assertive instead. Being nice enables others to get what they want. It doesn't get you what you want in life.

It's important to look at the other messages from the institutions that are influencing and reinforcing society's norms and shaping our children's futures.

For example, I attended a primary school play one day, with the set showing the interior of an aeroplane, the chairs set up in aisles. The mums and dads were cooing and waving to their young children as they were about to perform in the show and there was a real sense of anticipation. When it began, however, I was shocked at how the gender roles in an innocent play in a primary school pervaded.

ALL the girls were air hostesses. No boys were serving passengers. The only two boys were the pilots. In that moment, I thought what is going on here, is it a conspiracy?

I mentioned it to a mother next to me and she said, "Yes, it's terrible, isn't it?" The play was funny and the actors did a great job and we all gave them a huge clap of encouragement at the end.

We left shortly after, but on the way out I mentioned it to their class teacher. I said that I was shocked that in 2014, girls were still playing the subservient roles and boys were playing the leadership roles. She looked at me firstly like I was on another planet and then in an irritated way replied, "the children CHOSE those roles."

I was surprised that the children were 'reflecting' what was happening around them and also the teachers were replicating the status quo and not questioning the children's choices. I guess it is easier to repeat what they have always done, not question their choices and go along with the norm.

My presumption was that in post-feminist times, a teacher would be championing and questioning gender stereotyping, but unfortunately, they were further engendering our children and reducing the girls' aspirations.

In this environment, it doesn't take much imagination to envisage how this scenario is repeated many times every day and how and where gender stereotypes are reinforced.

Therefore, how do we enable our girls to rise above this pressure, stand up, follow their own paths and achieve their own dreams?

I've looked back and thought why I didn't push this further and perhaps speak to the head teacher to highlight and try to change this scenario. The truth is that I was rushing to get back to work after taking an hour off to see the play, the teacher looked worn out and I then got distracted by how I was going to get to my car in the rain and drive to work.

I should have had a chat with the head teacher, said what a fabulous job the children had done and that I was surprised that the girls were all playing one role and the boys were all doing another. I would then have asked if it was possible to instruct one girl to be a pilot and one boy to be a pilot and ensure there is equality in the roles next time. There could have been a class discussion about it or even an assembly to raise awareness.

I could have then followed it up with an email. Having it written down means that the school must follow the process for addressing any issues, so it would have been logged, addressed and investigated.
If your children are still at school, you could look out and email any inequalities that are going on in your child's school.

This scenario can be seen as a microcosm of our society today. You can see that the institutions that our children live in are traditional and are slow to change. These ideas cost nothing, but their value could mean a great deal in the wider world to our girls.

I ask that any teacher reading this revisit how they produce plays, assemblies and read texts and try their best to ensure equal representation which will then become the 'norm' in their classroom.

This is not in any way meant as a criticism. During lockdown we all got to see for ourselves our teachers in action on Zoom teaching sessions. I, for one, was in awe of our computer teacher as they explained how to write code. They explained it clearly, then had to repeat it for a pupil who wasn't concentrating and then again for a pupil who didn't understand it. The patience shown in those two instances was above and beyond what I could do myself. Thank you to them and to all teachers for bearing the responsibility for our childrens' futures.

When I was studying at university, I read that girls achieve better academically if they were in single sex schools. For boys it was the same in either type of school, as they are often louder and demand more attention from the teachers and girls are often left alone as they are quieter (cue life in the outside world).

I mentioned this to a teacher friend who said yes but "boys catch up in the outside world". It made me think, but do they? Do they catch up in the world outside school, or do good girls hang back, slow down or stand still, as they are told to do by society, making way for their less able peers to speak up more, demand more, achieve more and BE MORE?

Would you put your most talented, intelligent, skilled workforce in low skilled, low level menial jobs?

As a business this would have no logic and the business would soon come to a halt as employees would leave and there would be a skills shortage. In the outside world, this makes no sense either but it has become the norm in society.

Friends and Peers

When you are a teenager, you think you are different, but you are in reality, highly influenced by your peer group. It has been said that you are the sum of the five people you surround yourself with, creating your own norms and 'rules' as you navigate your role in the group and your path in life.

When I was at school, in the grammar school system, I wasn't focused enough on passing exams to be a serious scholar and I didn't know the value of the 'once in a lifetime opportunity' in the UK educational system.

Instead, I turned to the girls in my school year and was drawn to the girls who seemed to be having the most fun in class, enjoying the constant tension between the bright, fun girls and the teachers. Not many young girls can resist the lure of fun with their peers and living in the present, over facing the seriousness of choosing who to be, for the rest of their life?

We are constantly advised these days to 'live in the present' as a form of meditation. Don't think of what you should be doing but relax, breathe and enjoy the moment you are in. I have to say that this technique really works for me. As I take a deep slow breath in and out, I can feel after each one that my hunched, tightened shoulders are somehow less tight and fall down lower than the constantly tight state that seems to come with a modern, fast paced life.

Maybe we are naturally drawn to fun and stress relievers as a way of coping with life. What do you think?

It has been said that:

"Your friends really are your future. And the implication is that you don't just need to be more deliberate about who you're spending the most time with. You need to be examining your entire network of people and its influence on your life. You need to know where you sit inside the larger network of your social community." How to Win Friends and Influence People (Originally – Dale Carnegie (1936)).

Peers and other influencers play a huge role in our childrens' lives so you need to keep communicating with your children to find out where they are going, what they are thinking and who they are mixing with.

In the next chapter let's look at how women behave in the exterior world.

Ideas to Action

(1) What could your daughter achieve in the exterior world?

(2) Could you enable that?

(3) How long does she spend with friends in real life?

(4) Does she spend a long time looking at her phone?

(5) Do you think she has a positive body image?

(6) How can you endorse this?

(7) How can you role model a healthy body image?

(8) Can you encourage her to do activities where she sees normal people in real life?

(9) How did your teachers reinforce gender stereotypes?

(10) Did you ever question it?

Actions to Empower

(1) Have a chat with your daughter(s), son(s), niece(s) or nephew(s) about gender stereotypes in their school.

(2) Encourage them to critique how their school helps or hinders female equality.

(3) Ask them to question these roles in class, when preparing plays or assemblies.

(4) How could they challenge their friends when they see gender stereotyping?

(5) What are the gender stereotypes in your own life? How can you change these?

(6) What individual talents does your child have? Make a plan so they can put more time and effort into these.

(7) How can you encourage your child to think independently and not conform to global brand influences?

(8) Ask your child how they could ease pressure on themselves and their friends to be less focused on surface looks.

(9) Give yourself positive self-talk, such as "I did well to open the conversation today and learnt a lot."

(10) Pat yourself on the arm while you say it out loud, for positive reinforcement.

CHAPTER 5

Your Career

AFTER HAVING BEEN A 'good girl' at school and passing your GCSEs or A' Levels and even going to university, you quickly realise that these are purely tickets towards the end goal of choosing a career.

Are you motivated by status, cash or happiness?

Are you creative, good with numbers, good with words, good at talking on the spot? Have you got all the relevant qualifications, or will you need more?

Can you move, travel, or do you like to be near home?

Do you like to be indoors or outdoors?

You may need to balance what you love with how much you get paid, as many creative arts or charity sector jobs are interesting and rewarding, but don't pay as much.

As we live in a capitalist society, where your value as an individual is based on what you earn, what car you drive or what brand of bag you carry, this may have more importance to you too.

Now that you're forging your own individual identity, have a supportive group of friends and social life, your happiness will increase.

Applying for Jobs

You need to first write your CV and list all the relevant experience you have for each particular job.

This can be time-consuming but it is well worth the effort as each company wants to know why you want to work for them in particular and what relevant skills have you got for their particular job, so it is well worth the effort.

Have you asked around your circle of friends to see if they know of anyone hiring or go on LinkedIn to do a search and put your details online along with the role you are looking for.

You could also sign up to a job agency, so take your CV so you can meet them and they can remember you favourably, should a job come up and lots of people apply.

Interviews

Once you have secured an interview, then you need to practice your interview technique and one of the best is the STAR (Situation, Task, Actions, Results) technique of answering questions so use this framework when you answer any questions.

For example,

Situation – when I was speaking with customers.

Task - I had the difficult task of hearing from a customer who had waited 40 minutes for their order

Actions - I found out from the chef that it was going to be another 5 minutes.

Results - I told the customer the situation, apologised and brought it over as promptly as possible.

You should always do thorough research about the company and practice out loud with a friend or on video, until you are fully confident answering the question.

You should also be prepared to ask at least one question, such as, "How would you describe the company culture" as you want to know how you will fit in. Or "what training will I have?"

Save any questions about salary or holidays until you have been offered the job and then negotiate a higher salary for yourself.

Self-Development

If you are a member of a professional body and would like to progress in your career, then you may be part of a continuous personal development (CPD) programme. This aims to keep you up to date with your studies and knowledge and also helps you with your confidence.

Knowledge is power and you have something typed in black and white to show your progress, competency and level of study. If you suffer from self-doubt or imposter syndrome this is solid proof of your ability.

If you are NOT part of a programme like this, it is very easy to lose your way and lose your confidence in your abilities, so devise your own so that you can maintain some focus in your own life and career.

Imposter Syndrome

This has only fairly recently been identified and basically it means that once you have been given an opportunity in your career, then you may experience self-doubt as you move onwards and upwards and out of your comfort zone.

The little internal voice inside your head might say:

- You're not good enough.
- How did you even get this job?
- You're wrong.
- Everyone knows you're a fake.

These ideas might sometimes be fed by comments other people make, that may grow out of proportion or when you compare yourself to other more confident people, who seem to be self-assured or even from people who try to put you down to make themselves feel more powerful.

As you can see it's very complex, perhaps it was from your past experiences?

If you are experiencing self-doubt, then in the first instance, it's worth speaking to your friends and family to get some support and help quash those demons, or it may be worth speaking to a life or assertiveness coach. I personally found it very helpful to move towards my own goals.

This is so common amongst women and there is now a huge industry built around developing self-confidence in a supportive, feminine style, so you are not alone and should investigate festivals such as womanifest.co.uk founded by Assertiveness Coach, Jodie Salt.

Gain Confidence

I was told recently that if you want to gain confidence, then learn a new skill or do a course and get a qualification.

Education goes hand in hand with confidence. If you get the affirmation of a qualification, you can get a certificate and it is in black and white (and colour if you are lucky) for all to see.

There's a lot of actions you can take to increase it, so if you are lacking a bit of confidence, then please take small steps toward it.

You will surprise yourself; I promise.

Growth Mindset

If you need more skills and experience to get to the next step on the career ladder, then you need to develop a Growth Mindset.

Basically, it is a way of thinking that is being kind to yourself. Instead of beating yourself up internally saying negative self-talk like, "I am rubbish at this" you can re-frame those conversations with yourself and say, "I am not great at doing a spreadsheet... yet".

This gives you permission to not be fantastic at everything straight away and it also puts you in a position of growth, so that you can work towards your goals.

You then need to say to yourself, "How can I learn to use excel effectively?". This is manageable so you can either book yourself on a course or look it up on YouTube. You also learn a lot by doing the task as well and you should find out the best way that you learn either by looking, listening, reading or doing.

You may dream of a career that doesn't involve GCSEs, A Levels, a degree or a vocational course.

You may wish to pursue a role in the arts, as a performer, or anything else,

As a single woman with few commitments of a partner, children or responsibilities, this really is your opportunity to focus on and pursue your dreams.

Let's look how at successful women in society and what they have achieved, for inspiration.

Ideas to Action

1. What is your dream job?

2. Think of 5 things that you want in a job?

3. Think of 5 things you need in a job?

4. Think of 5 things you would hate in a job?

5. Think of all the roles with potentially good salaries.

6. Surround yourself with supportive people and ask lots of questions.

7. Develop a growth mindset and identify gaps such as "I am not great at this... yet."

8. Think about networking online or in real life with people who could help you get there.

9. Work hard at improving your skills.

10. Get a qualification in your chosen subject(s).

Actions to Empower

① Research what careers are well paid online (traditionally male dominated roles).

② Write a list of what skills you need to develop your career.

③ Find a career mentor who is doing the job you would like to do. Contact them and ask for their advice.

④ What experience, skills and qualifications could improve your career prospects?

⑤ When you decide on a course, email or ring them to enquire about the days, time, cost and any qualifications needed to start it.

⑥ If you are holding yourself back, invest in yourself and employ a life coach to develop your confidence and focus.

⑦ Volunteer to gain those skills to put on your CV.

⑧ Apply for at least 10 jobs or take 10 steps towards your own business.

⑨ Give yourself positive self-talk every day, such as "I am skilled at ....", or "I have many years' experience in ...."

⑩ Pat yourself on the arm while you say it out loud, for positive reinforcement.

CHAPTER 6

Successful Women

I COULDN'T WRITE A book about women and empowerment without mentioning some of the most successful women in the media who have endured the inequalities mentioned above.

Let's look at their achievements and how they have been treated in society over decades.

Marilyn Monroe

Having been obsessed with the image of Marilyn Monroe as a teenager, I devoured books on her life, her films and collected photographs of her glamorous Hollywood screen image.

She had a sad upbringing as her mother suffered from mental illness and she never knew her father. She spent many years in foster homes and dreamt of going to Hollywood where everyone would love her.

She was driven by a desire to be loved and became a victim of the brutal world of Hollywood where she was at the mercy of film directors and producers. She spent many times on the 'casting couch' exchanging sexual favours to realise her dreams.

She was beautiful, talented, she could sing and she wanted to be a serious actress, but the Hollywood machine wouldn't let her. They wanted her to look beautiful and act like a dumb blonde, realising men's fantasies. She played this role many times in films but she was anything but dumb.

Her image made Hollywood millions. It is said that she earned a lot of money for a lot of men but when she died, she didn't have enough money in her account to pay for her own funeral. She left 75% of her estate and intellectual property to her acting coach, Lee Strasberg and 25% to Dr Marianne Kris who was her psychiatrist and friend (*Yahoo Finance July 2023*).

She had spent many years trying to make it in films, by modelling nude amongst other jobs to survive. She was regularly invited to powerful men's houses in the film industry, in the hope that by charming them she could get a break into films.

They often promised to make her famous and one in particular invited her to his mansion to have dinner. She would have to undress and he would look at her and stroke her breasts while he told her stories of film stars he knew. This was quoted in the book 'Marilyn Monroe a Never-Ending Dream' Plexus Publishing Ltd, compiled and edited by Guus Luijters (1986). Look it up to find out more.

The man didn't make any call to give her a job or a break, he just kept on inviting her to dinner to look at her and stroke her. Shame on him.

Marilyn (born Norma Jean Baker) died aged 36 and became a Hollywood legend for her acting, beauty and potent sexual allure and this image still endures today. She was also witty, determined but powerless.

She had three husbands and two of them hated her career and Joe DiMaggio wanted her to be his wife full-time, but she wanted to keep her career. She said:

> *"I had always been nothing, a nobody. Then I had a chance to be somebody. I couldn't give it up, just when things were looking good for me. Not just to be a housewife, even Joe's housewife. I had to see if I could be a success on my own... After all I've been through, I won't quit now" - Marilyn Monroe.*

She was found dead naked and officially her cause of death was an overdose. However, since then rumours and theories of the real reason for her death and those involved have become rife and unresolved including her links with brothers, Bobby and John F Kennedy (who was President at the time of her death). She had previously complained of being passed around and used by them.

In 1951 she received the Henrietta Award for the 'Most Promising Personality of the Year'. In 1953 she received an award for 'Best Young Box Office Personality' for Gentlemen Prefer Blondes and the Photoplay Award for 'Fastest Rising Star of 1952'. In 1954 she won the Photoplay Award for 'Best Actress'. In March 1959 she won both the French Oscar for The Prince and the Showgirl and the Italian David di Donatella Prize. In 1960 she won the Golden Globe award for 'Some Like it Hot'. In 1962 she won the award for 'Most Popular Movie Star in the World'.

Fed up of playing dumb blondes, she formed her own company, Marilyn Monroe Productions Inc, with Milton Greene in 1955.

Joan and Jackie Collins

Joan Collins achieved fame at an early age in Hollywood in the 1950s and brought her sister along with her. Whilst there, Jackie met a host of Hollywood icons and her own experiences were not always good ones.

She decided to write about her experiences in a book where the main character, Lucky Santangelo, chose her own career and how to spend her personal life with the men she wanted having the sex she desired. It was a fantasy world where for once she was in control of her own life.

At the time of her books' publications, she was heavily criticized for her sexy style of writing. However, the masses (mainly women) thought differently. She wrote 32 books in her lifetime, all of which were New York Times best sellers in the 1980s and 1990s.

The Collins' sisters often portrayed as 'bitches' were anything but. They supported and enabled each other in their careers. When Joan became a Hollywood starlet at a young age, she got permission from her father, for her sister Jackie to accompany her.

Joan's career dipped after having children and Jackie returned the favour and cast her in 'The Stud' (1978), a film based on a sexy novel she had written in 1969. She was ultimately responsible for Joan's career rebirth.

The film was hugely successful and made $70m. The prequel made £7.5m in the box office and a further £1.5m in video rentals in the UK. They demonstrated a feminine style of collaborative working which was in part responsible for its success.

When Jackie visited Hollywood as a young girl, she had an affair with Marlon Brando, a hunky male movie star of the time, when he was 30 and she was 15. For this she received a lot of criticism, even though she was a naive young girl, new to Hollywood and he was in fact double her age! He was a seasoned idol at the time and well used to the Hollywood system and the 'perks' that he could enjoy. Surely this was not a fair and balanced relationship of equal parties. What would happen today?

Their parents, concerned about their 'wild' ways (blaming the girls, not the men who were trying to take advantage of them) made Jackie come home. However, it was too late, she had had the experiences and continued writing about the fantasy world where she had the power.

In the BBC TV documentary on the life of Jackie Collins, 'Lady Boss, the Jackie Collins Story', Director Laura Fairrie's take has revisited her as a feminist icon (2021).

The programme showed the difference that Jackie's husbands made in her life. Husband number one was a depressive who threatened to kill himself if she didn't stay with him. Eventually she left him as she couldn't live with the threat.

Husband number two, Producer Oscar Lerman, was a totally different partner and one day found some diaries she had written and could see that she was a talented writer. He asked her what her dream was and she said to go to Hollywood and write novels. He promptly moved them there and got her a book deal. He continued to build their dream home, even though he knew he was dying. What a hero.

Her third, younger husband had a big ego and was very jealous. He hated her success and writing, so she had to wake up in the night to write, or pretend to go to the bathroom to write, as he didn't like it. They eventually got divorced and he fought for her money. After that she swore never to marry again. She still got her book published despite him.

Her motto throughout her life was "girls can do anything" and she embodied that spirit in the female protagonists in her books and their willingness to fight for what they wanted.

Joan had five husbands and finally settled with Percy Gibson who was 32 years her junior. He fully supported her in her career and recently showcased her achievements in a Question and Answer for her latest book tour for "Behind the Shoulder Pads" where her quick wit proved she is still sharp as ever at the grand age of 90!

Madonna

Often described as the 'Queen of Pop', she is a song writer, singer, dancer, actress and performer. She is a role model who is independent, strong, creative, determined and has taken charge of her own sexuality, monetising it and making it in a man's world.

She is one of the most famous women in the world due to her imagination and work ethic. She credits her drive for attention, love and affection, on the untimely death of her mother.

She has starred in many films and documentaries including 'The Virgin Tour' where she said:

"I had a dream. I wanted to be a big star, I didn't know anybody, I wanted to dance, I wanted to sing, I wanted to do all those things, I wanted to make people happy, I wanted to be famous, I wanted everybody to love me. I wanted to be a star. I worked really hard, and my dream came true." - Madonna, 1985

The video of her tour alone went double platinum in sales, which means it sold more than 2 million copies.

I remember when she first appeared on 'Top of the Pops' in the 1980s with the song 'Like a Virgin' dressed as a bride. She was the main topic of conversation the next day at school as we had never seen a performance like it. She had expertly crafted a flirty sex appeal on screen, as well as being a talented song writer and performer.

By continuing to adapt and reinvent herself, she has charmed and flirted with the public and continues to fascinate the world in the present day.

Her next goal was to become an actress and she appeared in feature films such as 'Desperately Seeking Susan'. Despite scathing criticism about her acting from the media, she went on to play the lead role in the film 'Evita'. She took further singing and acting lessons and earned a Golden Globe Award for Best Actress in 1997 and in her acceptance speech said she hoped to "continue to be an artist, continue to perform and have more children."

She challenges our belief that women should not perform when they are older and has continued to maintain a high profile in her 60s.

On a personal level she is witty, eloquent and outspoken. Her song words are positive and inspiring with unforgettable lyrics and strident challenges. For example, in the song 'Express Yourself', she sang, "Don't go for second best baby, put yourself to the test!"

She is a feminist icon as she has actively fought against being put in a box due to her gender or age. She continues to be controversial and stretch the perception of how women should behave and what they should and could be.

Jennifer Lopez

Known as J-Lo. This woman is famous as a singer, dancer and actress.

She is the highest-paid Latina actress in the history of Hollywood, born in the Bronx from Puerto Rican descent. She started her career as an actress and later found success in the music industry with a series of popular albums.

Despite a hugely successful career as a singer, actress and performer she was heavily criticised and scrutinised by the Press in 2002 which put huge pressure on her relationship with the actor, Ben Affleck. Her career was subsequently portrayed as second to him and her achievements were second to his, despite the opposite being true in terms of the facts in record sales and box office successes.

After all the years of hard work, talent, pressure, persistence, determination, development of her image and stamina, in the end no matter what she had achieved, she was still perceived as second to the man she was in a relationship with. She was literally seconded.

What human would not be devastated, frustrated and enraged by this? The pressures of this led to the breakdown of her personal relationship. Ben and Jo-Lo ultimately rekindled their relationship and married in 2021. They are now regularly seen together in the media.

Katy Perry

In 2008 the energy and positivity Katy Perry put out from her first explosion into mainstream pop with the song 'I Kissed a Girl' made her a standout voice in the industry.

Despite her fun, kitsch videos, underlying this image is a fierce woman who has made it in a tough industry. She exudes feminist mantras such as in the song 'Roar'.

Her humour and positivity resonate throughout her many hits such as when she calls out her boyfriend in 'Hot n' Cold', questions her identity in 'Part of Me', channels the strength of an Egyptian Queen in 'Dark Horse' and even societal structures in 'Chained to the Rhythm'.

The song 'Firework' has an amazing chorus which acts like a rally call to action for us humans to realise our self-worth. Go and have a listen and see what you think.

Throughout her career, she has sold more than 48 million albums and singles, making her "one of the bestselling music artists of all time" (*Wikipedia, July 2023*) and the 6th greatest artist of all time (*Billboard, September 2021*).

The power of song writing is unquestionable and interestingly for women, song writing is a career that can be continued on maternity leave or worked around looking after children as long as you have the contacts, a supportive team and a forward-thinking record company,

It doesn't get more inspiring than that and honestly if you need a burst of energy and positivity, I urge you to put a Katy Perry playlist on, so that you can feel energised and empowered.

The Spice Girls

1994 was a pivotal year in feminist history due to the launch of five fearless females onto an unsuspecting world.

Victoria Beckham, Emma Bunton, Melanie Brown, Melanie Chisholm and Geri Halliwell combined their energies and were stronger together.

To date, the Spice Girls have sold around 100 million records worldwide, which makes them the bestselling girl group of all time, as well as one of the bestselling artists of all time.

"They achieved nine number one singles in the UK, spending 22 weeks at number one and 50 weeks in the top 10 UK music charts".
(David Houston, Cheshire Live on-line, 3 Feb 2022).

In the late 1990s, the Spice girls became the faces of modern Pop Culture, with their female take on songwriting and performing. They were everywhere and on everything from TV programmes to Pepsi cola.

Back in 1995 when the pop phenomenon was rising, I too was looking for inspiration, when the job market was tough and I had just left university. The Spice Girls showed strength in numbers and as a group of five they were primed to show (off) their talents in performing and talking.

At a time when there was a lull and a lack of female role models, their energy was invigorating and inspirational and it should not be under-estimated. I even wrote my first published article about them back in the day for a graduate magazine called No.10.

Everyone had their favourite Spice Girl and I have to say that I looked up to Scary and Ginger for their strength, wit, energy and determination. They had all that and they were fun and gorgeous. Who wouldn't want to be that? Who is your favourite Spice girl?

In contrast to my own life, I landed back into the world of work in a PR job where the male owner was intent on making me feel undervalued.

He told my peer "Don't tell her she's good or she'll ask for a pay rise!". Not what a feminine style of leadership is all about, no wonder I was confused.

These were the days where entering Gentlemen's clubs was the height of success as a man and women were only just allowed to go in them. In truth, I did get to go into one of those oak panelled 'gentleman's clubs' and it was very dull, musty and outdated.

The contrast with what I experienced was stark to a young woman about to start her career and make some serious life choices for the first time.

I must admit the soundtrack of 'Spice up Your Life', 'All you Need is Positivity', 'Wannabe', and 'Tell Me What You Really, Really Want' played in my head on constant repeat as I chose a career to go for.

They inspired a generation of young women in the 90s and continue to inspire me to this day.

To celebrate their amazing achievements, in 2021 Channel 4 put out a three-part documentary series called 'How Girl Power Changed Britain'. This was to mark the anniversary of 25 years since their album 'Spice' was released in March 1994.

Britney Spears

Started her performing career on The Mickey Mouse Club and at 15 she released her first single and so her singing career began. She is often referred to as the 'Princess of Pop' and revived teen pop music in the 1990s and 2000s.

She has sold over 100 million records worldwide (including 70 million in the US). She is one of the world's bestselling music artists. She has earned a Grammy Award, 15 Guinness World Records, 6 MTV Music Video Awards, a Radio Disney Award, has a Hollywood Walk of Fame star, as well as numerous other awards and accolades (*Wikipedia September 2023*).

However, her longevity and success in the business has been clouded by her personal life, as Britney has endured a court ruling under a 13-year conservatorship. Due to concerns about her mental health, control of her personal and financial decisions was given to her abusive father, including her birth control (not allowing her to have her coil taken out when she wanted a baby).

The clues were in her shows and Instagram account where she was often seen in a cage. She was touring the world, producing an album and earning millions of dollars, but according to the law, she remained 'unfit' to make her own personal and financial decisions.

Luckily for Britney, her super fans picked up that 'something was not right' and started a powerful campaign called #FREEBRITNEY. This took years to take effect, but eventually raised the issue of how Britney was being enslaved by her father.

I thank those fans who were mocked and disbelieved. They had determination and belief in their gut feelings and I know that Britney has thanked them in her book. It demonstrates how important it is to trust your 'gut' feeing and we should all do this more.

TV documentaries continued the campaign and cast light on her bullying father and the legal trap she was in, ultimately turning Britney's life around.

Britney had tried many times but was threatened that if her dad was not the conservator, (supposedly acting in her best interests) then the new one replacing him would be the court's choice and this could work out even worse. This situation meant that Britney's own money paid for her virtual imprisonment and lack of freedom to make her own choices.

When trying to prove she was capable of running her own affairs, the legal system proved extremely difficult to get out of and despite appealing, she was not listened to.

Eventually Britney gave her own testimony in 2021. As a result of the court hearing, the Judge allowed her to choose her own lawyer and sack her old one. She had been paying for her own lawyers, the music industry lawyers, the court lawyers and her family lawyers. Once in court, evidence was given on how she was coerced and controlled by her father, who allegedly bribed her by threatening she wouldn't be allowed to see her two children.

He also had medical professionals put her on lithium (a strong medicine used to control mood disorders such as depression and bi-polar disorder). Wouldn't you be depressed if you couldn't choose to go out in your car without pre-arranging it with a team, couldn't have a baby or couldn't spend your own money?

On further investigation, her father's father was similarly controlling. History was repeating itself. The Sheriff had once found one of his wife's bodies at the grave of a child that had died eight years earlier and was told she had post-natal depression. It was recorded that she had committed suicide by shooting herself in the chest with her own foot.

Her grandfather also had a history of locking his wives up in mental institutions and putting them on lithium to control them, so her father had learnt all he needed to know from him.

However, the good news is that:

> *"After 13 years, she is regaining control of her own personal and financial situation and has released a new record."* (Article in New York Times by Dana Kennedy, 9 October 2021).

She has also written her own book called 'The Woman in Me' to rave reviews in October 2023.

Taylor Swift

Has written 13 top selling albums and tens of chart busting songs in the UK, US and around the world. She has penned many songs about strong women and has even used her voice to write songs in response to the media writing stuff about her. She has used her genius to answer back to her many critics as an on-going dialogue with the press, to the untruths written about her, about the untruths written about the men she has gone out with, who dumped who and why. She has taken on many female personas which have stretched the tight constraints of what women are *'allowed'* to feel and *'allowed' to do* without fear, despite often receiving a torrent of criticism along the way, especially about her love life.

She turned it to her advantage and ultimately triumphed over her darkest moments and flipped them to songwriting success and critical acclaim. Singing about revenge and playing the game of love, with theatrical themes of red and bloodshed add to her power, strength and dominance. I feel like I have been on her life's journey with her as she tackles taboo subjects of feeling joy at getting revenge, of not being a victim, taking personal responsibility for making bad choices, of learning to set boundaries and respecting herself.

She also writes about being honest, feeling angry, feeling powerful, being empowered to retaliate and not become a victim, which can disempower and destroy us.

Her performances, humour and talent for writing catchy tunes are legendary. She is a powerful force and role model to speak her truth. Her influence in the music industry has stretched to world politics and beyond as she has even opposed Trump using her platform.

She sings, plays guitar, banjo and piano, composes music set to the narrative poetry she has written. As a woman she has demonstrated a gamut of emotions from vulnerable to vengeful.

Her open dialogue with fans on her platforms, connecting emotionally on common ground, shows that she listens and she speaks up.

She has been criticised in the media for having too many boyfriends, not having a boyfriend, being too thin, too fat and too vocal but her talent is unquestionable.

I've never heard a derogatory word for a man having too many girlfriends. Have you? A man is simply described as 'playing the field' or 'spreading his wild oats'.

However, she has still performed at her fastest selling world tour in 2023 where tickets are going on re-sale for £750 each, such is the demand to see her.

It has been said that "Taylor IS the music industry" (*Barbara Walters, 2014*) because of the power she holds.

The England Women's Euro 2022 Squad

Made up of Manager Sarina Wiegman, Captain Leah Williamson, Vice Captains Ellen White, Lucy Bronze, and Millie Bright. Alessia Russo, Alex Greenwood, Bethany England, Beth Mead, Chloe Kelly, Demi Stokes, Ella Toone, Ellie Roebuck, Fran Kirby, Hannah Hampton, Jess Carter, Jill Scott, Keira Walsh, Lauren Hemp, Lotte Wubben-Moy, Mary Earps, Nikita Parris, Rachel Daly, (Support from Georgia Stanway, Katie Zelem, Lucy Staniforth, Niamh Charles, Sandy MacIver and Steph Houghton).

In 2022, England's female football team became Champions of Europe.

It was one of the most exhilarating games ever seen. Ella Toone scored first for England against Germany, then Lina Magull's 79th minute goal for Germany equalised the teams. This forced the match into extra time with Chloe Kelly finally scoring for England again, saving us all from the heart-stopping moments of a penalty shoot-out!

The public impact of the game meant that the tube in London was packed from midday with people wearing their England shirts. It was flooded with fans and a carnival atmosphere ensued in London which hadn't been achieved since 1966.

In the rest of the country, we as a nation collectively felt the nerves and saw the determination over adversity, play out in front of our very eyes during the match. We saw the huge hearts of our Lionesses, as they came back again and scored. We ultimately triumphed.

"It was gutsy, exhausting and exhilarating", according to Suzanne Wrack of The Guardian (*Sunday, 31 July 2022*). It was an emotional journey for us all and men cried at the sheer drama and emotions played out throughout the game. It was, literally, a watershed moment for many.

The Lionesses have shown us the way and the future for all women. Women seen at their fittest on national TV, with huge audiences, scoring goals and coming back to win heroically. To become champions of Europe, supported by the whole of London at Wembley stadium, at home, with record numbers of viewers in real time and again on catch up TV.

They attracted a record crowd of 87,192 spectators at Wembley. You simply can't argue against those numbers.

This match is a reboot in the revolution for women.

I am still taking it in. This is a seminal moment for women's football, women's sports and the female struggle for respect and equality. It also highlighted the fact that, despite this achievement, many of the women still had their other full-time jobs. The struggle for equity continues.

All of the above women are championing their causes. The creative arts and sports fields are proven to be available to us. Would you like to leave a legacy? What could it be?

Nadine Merabi couldn't make clothes when she started out, but she had a dream to be a designer and so set out to learn. Now her unique clothes are worn by celebrities all over the world.

Are you a talented designer, singer, dancer or athlete? You have to start somewhere, so take a step to realise your potential today. All the above successful women started locally performing, drawing or writing at home or in their bedrooms. Why not you?

If you cannot find that club, team or hobby that you'd like to do, then put it on Facebook or other social media and start your own group. If you want to do it and can't find it, the chances are that there will be a lot of other people who feel the same. Go girl!

In the next chapter we will look at your identity - past, present and future.

Ideas to Action

1. Are you creative?

2. Can you write a song?

3. Can you sing?

4. Can you play an instrument?

5. Can you write a story or a poem?

6. Can you design an outfit?

7. Can you perform an act?

8. Can you dance?

9. Can you play a sport?

10. What else can you do?

Actions to Empower

① Put on your favourite feminist songs so you feel empowered, which are

② Dance to your favourite songs.

③ Sing a song loudly.

④ Play an instrument, practice it until you are confident and record it.

⑤ You may have put on shows for your family as a child, can you perform an act now at your local pub or venue?
Many are looking for entertainment for their customers, so ask them!

⑥ Write a short story or article about a subject you are passionate about called

⑦ Send your story or article to at least five magazines or newspapers whose audience would appreciate it, to get feedback.

⑧ Design an outfit and either make it or get a dressmaker to make it for you.

⑨ Give yourself positive self-talk, such as "I was really creative today."

⑩ Pat yourself on the arm while you say it out loud, for positive reinforcement.

CHAPTER 7

Your Identity

WOMEN OFTEN STRUGGLE WITH their identity and no wonder, as it has been systematically changed throughout their lives.

We may start out with one name, but it is changed and we are given a new name after each life event. Our original name, identity and individuality then become a ghost in the past.

You may start life as Jennifer Jones (name is given to you), then you may gain a qualification or two or have letters after your name, (all good) and you can choose to use it and put it on your business card. Then you may get married and you are expected to take on the name of your new spouse. You may be strong and keep your own name or you may opt to go traditional and be Mrs Smith. Or you may choose a combination of both names and go double-barrelled.

If you do opt to change your name, as a rite of passage, you must then complete all the relevant paperwork for your passport, send off your marriage certificate and wait for a new one to come back, with a new photo and a new name.

You must then notify all the companies that you pay bills to, your mortgage company, the DVLA for your driving licence, the doctor, the dentist and the list goes on and on.

Then you may decide to have children and your new name is no longer Mrs Smith, or Jenny. It's now Joe's Mum.

From the following list, circle how many roles you carry out at the moment:-

Accountant	Entertainer	Operations
Banker	Expert	Manager
Budgeter	Fact Checker	Partner
Cleaner	Friend	Personal
Cheerleader	Housekeeper	Shopper
Chef	Job (Outside	Physiotherapist
Coach	the Home)	Planner
Confidante	Lover	Project Manager
Counsellor	Masseuse	Social Secretary
Creative	Mood Buffer	Strategist
Daughter	Mother	Taxi Driver
Director	Organiser	Tidier
		Tutor
		Wife

What roles did you choose? What roles didn't you choose?

The Media

Outside of your home, if you read the news, a woman is usually described like so:

> Jenny Jones, age, hair colour, body shape - usually by how she looks or feels.

For example: Jenny Jones, 35-year-old slim blonde.

Whereas a man is described as:

> Mr Jonathan Jones, age, occupation - usually by what he does.

For example, Architect.

MailOnline

Loved-up Sienna Miller, 40, and her model boyfriend Oli Green, 25, put on a smitten display as they cuddle up at star-studded charity bash

By LAURA PARKIN FOR MAILONLINE
PUBLISHED: 01:59, 6 May 2022 | UPDATED: 06:00, 6 May 2022

Article in Daily Mail Newspaper, Laura Parkin, Femail: 6 May 2022

These descriptions say a lot about how a woman and how a man are viewed and defined, even in the 21st century! How would you want to be described?

It is no wonder that women are fixated on age, looks and feelings, rather than what they do. If you look at this article and many others like it, men are often defined by what they do.

This reflects the years of female socialisation of how they look or 'should' look and how men are and 'should' be. The focus is on what a woman looks like, or her emotions rather than what she has achieved as a form of status.

She may be the most intelligent, witty and fun woman in history, we would never know, as she is simply described as blonde, 35, slim.

Individuality

Even though we are under immense pressure to conform, the people who are their true selves come across as authentic and this is one of the most valued traits in a human being.

We watch social media videos and we measure their reach and the ones that go viral are the ones that are real. Do you remember the video where the young girl speaks to her sister and her tag line was, "Thanks a lot Rachel?"

As social proof of this, the video received 20 million views and 1.1 million Likes on YouTube. It is memorable even though it was 8 years ago or more.

It is a paradox that we are taught to conform and fit in, but those people who are true to themselves are the ones that stand out and are valued the most for their personality.

Therefore, take a risk and if you've got something to say, say it! Be brave and be your true self.

For a long time, I thought I needed to be 'nice' to fit in with what a girl should be. I had all these thoughts going on in my brain, but the overarching thought was don't be big headed, be seen and not heard and be liked (despite me not liking what had been said).

I've learned that you have to trust yourself and be in touch with what you are thinking and feeling. To do this you sometimes have to ignore what negative people say about you.

The reality is that when you do use your voice, it will spark a conversation, it will make others think and it will inspire others to speak too. How wonderful is that?

In the next chapter, let's look at how you can be your individual self and do what you like doing.

Ideas to Action

① What name were you born with?

② Did you change your name?

③ Why?

④ What name do you prefer?

⑤ Describe the person who has your first given name.

⑥ Describe the person with your married name.

⑦ Are you now "Mum of.."?

⑧ Who has more energy?

⑨ Which name makes you feel like your true self?

⑩ Which name makes you feel empowered?

Actions to Empower

(1) Correct people who call you "Joe's Mum" to your preferred name.

(2) What roles in your life can you delegate?

(3) What roles can you drop?

(4) What roles would you like to have?

(5) How would you like to be described?

(6) What would you like to say to your parents?

(7) What would you like to say to your children?

(8) What is individual about you?

(9) Make a 30 second video introducing yourself.

(10) When you are happy with it, post it on social media and start a trend.

CHAPTER 8

Your Hobbies

WHEN I WAS YOUNGER, I liked to run fast and at one point I was the only girl playing in a 5-a-side football team of 20+ year old men.

I would say that I felt free, fulfilled, positive, had banter with my male friends and had a good social life, as we often went to the pub afterwards for a post-match analysis.

When I look back, I was at my best physically, toned, fit, my skin glowed, I smiled and laughed a lot as endorphins (exercise hormones) ran through my body. I was fully confident. It strikes me that as humans we are programmed to gain pleasure for being healthy, as a reward for being fit for survival.

Running around makes you feel free, it's you living in the moment, not caring about what you're wearing, what you look like or how good your hair looks, so it's freeing physically and mentally. You can feel like a child again as you enter the childlike state of running around for fun.

What I didn't realise at the time was that these side effects were as important as playing the game itself. There are a number of key benefits and skills of doing a team sport which have stood me in good stead for the future. I would highly recommend it.

If you've had years of supporting your family, the chances are that you have let your hobbies go, so put some focus on yourself and reconnect to the person you once were, as they are integral to your identity.

You could start by picking hobbies that you can book and be there on time, to get you into the habit of thinking and planning for yourself. Do you love dancing? Book a Zumba class. Not to lose weight, just for the absolute joy of it.

Benefits

The benefits of playing a team sport are:

1. **New Skills** – I wasn't the most skilled, but I wasn't the worst either. However, I managed to move a ball around with no problems, so try it for yourself.

2. **Body-Confidence** - I felt really confident in my body as it was literally the best it could look. My legs were toned, my stomach was toned and I was

burning the calories and had a high metabolism, so could eat and drink what and when I liked.

3. **Networking** - I met some really good men in the team and we swapped information on what was happening locally (bands etc), recommendations for local tradespeople, best places to go and arranged nights out.

4. **Saving money** - I even managed to get a discount when I had my bathroom done as one of the guys was a tiler and tiled my bathroom.

5. **Teamwork** - we worked well as a team. It felt good to be one part of a whole unit with the same aims.

6. **Fitness** - I felt at my physical best, I could run upstairs, carry Christmas trees and even do heavy DIY jobs.

7. **Positivity** - I had loads of positive energy, which radiated out especially after the game when the feel-good factor of exercise takes effect.

8. **Respect** - I did feel a bit weird when I turned up and I was the only girl, but as I could run fast and help the team, I was considered one of the team.

9. **Happy** - pounding up and down a pitch made me feel exhilarated as the air blew against my face and my body flew through the air.

10. **Low cost** - we split a one-hour pitch cost; it was less than the price of a drink.

So, taking account of all the benefits above, why don't we all do more sports like this?

Men tend to have a few hobbies which they continue post children. They may play football, go cycling or climb mountains. It gets them out of the house and out of a boring routine.

As their life in the exterior world continues, women tend to replace their own hobbies with their children's so their lives become more insular. Have you fallen into this habit?

I've come to realise that having a hobby is important because it gives you an identity too. After all, you are what you do.

If you've lost your identity and want to invigorate yourself, here's some ideas if you are stuck:

Ideas

Photography - take a picture with your phone, print it and put it on your walls, or give it to a friend or family member to put something unique and personal on their walls. Don't forget to sign and date it so they remember you. You could also send them to a magazine, shop or gallery where you will get paid or at least a photo credit and can even build your CV/portfolio. You can get a lot of free or low-cost printing via apps like FREEPRINTS and delivery is fast too.

Sketching - have your pencil and pad near you, ready for when you have the opportunity or inspiration. Take 20 minutes or an hour so that you can draw something either in front of you or in your mind's eye, that's inspired you or that interests you. Like those flowers? Draw them before they die.

Painting - If you like painting, then have the paints, brushes, water and paper at the ready for when you have those 20 or 60 minutes in the evening, to do just a little bit or even a lot, if you have the time. Time flies when you are having fun, so you may get lost in it. If you have a spare table, leave your tools out so that you can dip in and out and you have a reminder as you can see them there, ready and waiting for you.

If you haven't got a table, use a big sheet of cardboard, have the tools ready on it and simply pull it out from under the coffee table, sofa or bed and spend some blissful time being creative, doing what you love, in your own happy place and simply being you.

Writing - If you like writing, then set yourself 20 minutes to do some, put it on a timer if you need to and get into the zone where you can type or write, or make notes and jot down thoughts in your phone or notepad when an idea pops into your head, so that you've got a starting point to expand on.

Don't get too distracted by going on your phone and stick to your writing notes. Practice makes perfect so keep honing your skills until you are happy to show them to someone.

Craft - do you like to make cards, clothes or cushions? Then do so, if you think about it, you have 7 days in the week. Surely you can calve out 20 minutes a day so that you are moving forward and doing something you enjoy, for yourself and letting your creativity run riot.

Using this part of your brain helps with stress relief, helps you to be calmer and it also gives your brain a rest from forever multi-tasking, as you focus on the task at hand.

Visit the Theatre or Cinema – look online to see what's on near you, ask some friends and book it! If there's a show you've wanted to see for ages then ask someone to buy you tickets for your birthday or Christmas and go together. You can do this even when the weather's bad and it can really cheer you up on a Winter's evening.

Self-Defence Classes - There are a few types of self-defence classes such as Ju Jitsu and Karate which can help you get fit, if you don't mind being one on one with a partner.

Ask friends, family or acquaintances if they know of any. Use Facebook groups or Google your local class to book a trial to see if you like it, the people and the overall vibe.

You should feel a lot stronger and more confident after this, which will permeate into other areas of your life.

Zumba Dance - This became a craze in the noughties and classes still continue. Again, Google or ask around for local classes or do a search on Facebook for Zumba to see what's available.

When are you more likely to go?

- in the evening (when there's someone to mind the kids)
- first thing in the morning to get your day off to a good start or
- in the afternoon to give you energy for when you pick up the children?

It's surprising but taking exercise really does give you more energy.

The added benefits of physical activities are tenfold in my experience, it gets you out of the house. This is a bonus as you get to see what is going on in the real world outside your own box.

If you go in your car you get to experience great music of your choice such as 90s dance or 80s floor fillers. This, in itself, gets you in a good mood, as you can choose the music you like, or sing your heart out in the car and be transported to 'back in the day'.

If you are close enough to walk to your local leisure centre or sports club, then you should leave a bit early so you can experience the real-life senses of sight and smell, as you feel the sensations and distractions of nature and live in the present (without going on your mobile phone).

Or, you could even put noise cancelling headphones on and listen to your favourite energising play list. The world can be a noisy place these days, with people lost in their own thoughts or speaking loudly to their friends, without a thought for the impact their noise has on other people. Focus on what you like and want to listen to and give yourself some choice and calm. Please take extra care when crossing roads though.

Another bonus is that you might find your 'tribe' of people who are interested in the same hobby as you.

I'd do a trial on this too as some classes call themselves Zumba which is originally from Columbia and uses music deriving from Latino samba and merengue dances. However, I've been to a couple that play hard house with high intensity dance moves instead. It might help to revisit a class that you used to like back in the day to see if you still like it, or try something completely new.

As a teenager I used to dream of being a backing dancer on Top of the Pops. These days I try and attend a weekly dance class led by a brilliant choreographer called Jonathan Chianca who teaches us all the moves from iconic female singers such as Madonna, Beyonce and J Lo. Not only do you get to listen to your favourite music, but you also get to dance, have fun, raise your heartbeat, tone your body and hang out with like-minded people.

Racquet sports – if you've ever liked racquet sports such as table tennis, badminton or tennis, these also offer the benefits of being very sociable as you can play in singles or doubles and in a good club you will probably end up going for coffee, learning about other people's lives and developing your skills on the court.

My mother always loved tennis, but working two jobs and bringing me up, ensured it was on the back burner for a while, but once she retired, she took it up again. She regularly wins medals for player of the month and has just been asked to join a new club. She never thought she was good enough, but to be asked to join because of her abilities was a real confidence boost to her and an inspiration to me. I know what I'm going to try when I am older!

Horse riding – I tried this only once, riding bare back on holiday, but many girls become obsessed with horse riding when they are young. They even muck out the stables too (can't understand that personally) but they say there is something to be said for riding and steering a powerful beast at your own speed for clearing your head. If you used to do this as a child or teenager, it may be worth re-booking a riding class to literally get you back in the saddle.

Running - the benefit of running is that you can do it any time of the day, for however long you want and go whenever you feel like it. All you need is a decent pair of trainers. If like some women you don't feel quite safe running on your own, or you are not sufficiently motivated on your own, then it might be worth asking at least one friend to buddy up with, so you can run together. You can then set some targets of how far, or how fast you would like to go, raise your heartbeat, tone up and get those happy endorphins coursing through your veins. There are lots of running clubs that meet locally at various times and are sociable too.

Some people go on to sign up for half or full marathons, so that they have a deadline to get fit for. There are always running events such as Pretty Mudder that are linked to charities, so you also get to raise money for a good cause if you need an added incentive.

Voluntary work - I'm channelling my mother here as she has volunteered at various charity shops. The benefits are you become a member of the community, positively contribute to it and can be creative if you wish to dress the shop window which is high on Maslow's hierarchy of needs (see Chapter 9). Or you can use your brain for counting the day's takings and get motivated to hit the shop's sales targets. You can also meet like-minded people who want to give back to the community and give up their valuable time for a good cause close to their heart. I guarantee this will make you feel good about yourself as well as learn new skills.

Charity shops are always looking for reliable volunteers to work at the till, or behind the scenes in the back, sorting through valuable donations, steaming clothes, putting them on hangers and pricing them ready for sale. I did this when I lived abroad and only had a visitor's visa which was invaluable in helping me integrate into a new country.

Just call into your local charity shop, ask for details about working there and offer your services. Even if it is for half a day a week or a day per month, they will put you on to their rota of voluntary staff. You would be amazed at what is donated by people, from wedding dresses to wardrobes and you may even get a discount on items for sale on working there.

If you are out of practice or have had a career break, you can update your CV ready for your next paid role.

If you always liked pets but don't have the time and money to have your own, then you could volunteer at the local vets or pet sanctuary. Beware of your own limitations though before you go, as if you love animals, you may find yourself adopting one or more.

I can also recommend an excellent charity called Girls Out Loud which seeks to empower young girls and will empower you in the process, with monthly meetings and 3 monthly training, led by award-winning Jane Kenyon and her wonderful team.

You could ask your work to sponsor you for a year or you could sponsor yourself.

Follow and message them on Instagram @GirlsOutLoudOrg to find out more.

I hope the above ideas have sparked your interest in life outside of working hard and minding children, as a virtual reality world of social media can be pretty insular. They have their benefits of course, but like anything, a balanced lifestyle is more beneficial for your well-being, so you enjoy being your own individual self in the real world, keep your communication skills honed to perfection and your relationships real.

Tips

Put your dance clothes or sports bag out the night before, so that you are physically and mentally prepared. After all, that's a step towards getting there. Once you are in the kit, you are more inclined to go.

Give yourself time to get ready in the morning so there are no barriers to actually getting out the door.

You might be like me as every time before I go I think, "Do I have to go?" and even "Do I really feel like it?" before I do any exercise, but I am always pleased during and afterwards, when the endorphins kick in. In fact, I miss it when I don't go as it keeps me feeling positive and uplifted. I am sure it will be the same for you.

Health

According to the NHS website www.nhs.uk (August 2022) exercise is "the miracle cure" for long term health too as it can "reduce your risk of major illnesses such as coronary heart disease, stroke, type 2 diabetes and cancer and lower your risk of early death by up to 30%" so it is worth investing the time for you and your family.

If you prefer more flexibility than a set class, you can walk, jog, run, subscribe to a YouTube Channel such as @TheFitnessMarshall (if you want to get fit, laugh and have fun) or even dance in your kitchen.

If you need to stretch or de-stress, then join a yoga group. You can attend classes online or even go on a yoga retreat organised by professionals such as Lyndsey Holden @positivevibesyoga.

It is flexible so you can:

- Relax immediately
- Get instant relief by stretching
- Do it inside or outside
- At a time to suit you
- Choose your own pace
- Make it easy or more challenging
- And it can be low-cost or free.

Furthermore, research shows that it can boost your self-esteem, your mood, your sleep quality and energy levels as well as reducing stress, depression, dementia and Alzheimer's disease" - *NHS website (August 2022)*.

If exercise was a pill, it would be the single most effective treatment for good health.

The evidence is overwhelming and it is recommended that adults should do 150 minutes of physical activity per week, through various activities from walking to sports.

What's more, adults now spend around seven hours per day sitting or lying down and the inactivity of a sedentary lifestyle while watching TV, working from home on a laptop or staring at your mobile phone, has been described by the UK Department of Health and Social care as 'a silent killer'.

So you can see there are even more reasons to exercise.

Music

Music is a powerful force and can heal, energise, soothe, empower and inspire you so make it a priority to listen to.

As a teenager I listened to music and learnt the song words of the latest hits from a magazine called Smash Hits. These days I simply type the song title into Google and the song lyrics as well as the video comes up almost instantly so I can sing along too.

You could put together a playlist of your favourite songs on your Spotify app to sing your heart out, as suggested by Jayne Bailey, who said it really makes her feel good and it's now the first thing I do when I get into my car.

Make it a priority to listen to! It can be the soundtrack to your life, so take control and choose some inspirational songs that empower and energise you on your journey.

Now that you have re-examined your present identity and reclaimed your hobbies, let's look at your options for the future.

Ideas to Action

1. If you want to feel fit and confident, ask yourself what sport have you always wanted to try?

2. What hobbies do you love (or did you love) that you could start (or re-start)?

3. Can you prioritise it and do it weekly for a happy and healthy life (day or evening)?

4. Research classes in your local area.

5. Ask a friend for recommendations.

6. Check Facebook for local groups.

7. You could get a buddy so you can motivate each other.

8. Or go alone if you wish to meet new people.

9. Try an online dance class.

10. Or dance in your kitchen whenever you want.

Actions to Empower

1. Research what kit you need to start your new hobby.

2. Buy kit, such as yoga mat, trainers etc, to feel motivated.

3. Get practical support, such as minding the kids.

4. Get encouragement if necessary.

5. Contact the organiser to ask any questions.

6. Book online.

7. Turn up and give it your best shot.

8. Keep going for at least 10 weeks so it forms a habit.

9. Give yourself positive self-talk, such as "I went totally out of my comfort zone to do yoga but I loved it."

10. Pat yourself on the arm while you say it out loud, for positive reinforcement.

CHAPTER 9

Your Future

IF YOU GOT IN a car, sat in the driving seat, fastened your seat belt, switched on your sat nav system and simply pressed 'you choose' as your destination, where would you expect to go? I'm 99% sure it wouldn't take you where you wanted to go. You would think I was mad for even suggesting it.

Chances are it would have taken you to an entirely different destination. Yet we switch on the TV and flick through the first few channels or pick up a magazine regularly that tells us to wear this, see this, buy this, do this.

Therefore, you are absorbing other people's ideas of who you should be and what you should do. These are based on old-fashioned ideas and agendas, for stuff you don't even need. We have been brainwashed since we were born into believing girls are like this and boys are like that. It's not set in stone for all time, it's changeable.

What I am saying, and I am on that journey too, is that we need to NOT adapt to our society, we need to CHANGE our society for ourselves, for our partners, for our daughters and for our sons.

Maybe you are feeling a little stuck on what you want, so look back at your achievements and you will see that you have triumphed over a lot of adversity through hard work, focus and determination, so you can use those qualities again and again throughout your life to get what you want.

Vision Board

I first heard about vision boards from Angela Florence Bentley and it opened my eyes to how limited my former aspirations were and introduced me to the possibilities I never knew were there in life.

A vision board is a visual representation and prompt of what you would like your dream future to contain such as publishing of a book or a goal to start your own company.

All you need is a large piece of cardboard, glue, magazines, glitter, coloured felt tips, scissors, ribbon, wrapping paper, coloured paper and old cards. In fact, anything that you love that you can stick down, or things that you have seen in a magazine that you would like to strive for.

Follow the steps below to create your vision board:

1. Take yourself into a space where you can lay out all your bits and bobs.

2. Cover the cardboard with your favourite wrapping paper.

3. Add a title like 'Vision Board 202...'

4. Then add all the visual images, or words that really speak to you from the magazines.

5. Make it as colourful, fun and eye-catching as possible.

6. Put your wildest dreams on it. For example, pictures of books or authors you admire.

7. Cut out words from magazines that speak to you like 'write'.

8. Stick on stars, colours, glitter or anything that you really love to make it a visual joy.

9. Put it on a wall where you will see it every day.

10. Look at it every day and you will consciously and subconsciously readjust your mindset to focus on those images which then focuses your mind to achieve them.

Take a picture and let me know on Instagram @iamjoannalambe how you get on, I would LOVE to know!

Time Management

Women are under huge pressures to conform but can you re-balance how you spend your time, maybe 20% on looking good enough and 80% on what you can achieve?

Only YOU know what you want, where you want to go, why you want to get there, who you need alongside you, how you can get there and when. Start today or tonight. Switch off the TV, put down the phone and sit there and ask yourself some questions. (Write it down on paper, not on your phone as you'll get distracted!

YOU get to choose, so it in a relaxing corner as you need to think clearly and decide where YOU want your life to go.

Don't get distracted by thinking about what your partner, your children, your friends, your family or your boss wants or needs.

And don't be too hard on yourself. You've had days, weeks, months, years and decades of being told what you 'should' do, so it might take a little time to dig deep and decide what is best for you.

The good news is that if you ask your brain a question, it is exactly like a computer and it will come up with an answer. Therefore, ask yourself the right questions before you go to bed. For example, "What do I want to achieve in my life?" and let your computer do its thing.

Sometimes trying to figure out what you want to achieve in your life is difficult, so you may find it easier to start with what you don't want.

This is so important as we women need to know what we want and when we want it and use our voices more often to ask for it.

We need to be able to get what we want and do what we want without feeling ashamed, selfish or guilty about it.

We also need to practice communicating what we want. For example, "I would like you to ...."

"I am spending time on my own project, so can you do ...."

"You spend two nights a week doing your hobby, so I am spending two nights a week doing mine. I think this is fair."

Good Habits

Once you start doing this, you will gain respect, you might get agreement and you might be surprised. Women asking for what they want is empowering for women, it is also empowering for men. They then know exactly what you need or want, without trying to work it out themselves, so it's a win-win situation.

Start today or start tonight but think about what you want and then think about how you are going to say it. If you are not used to asking for what you want, you might need to practice it in your head first, then out loud a couple of times so you get more comfortable with it.

When you have your answer to "what do I want?" you need to decide how you are going to get there, so let's plan to use the SMART technique (Specific, Measurable, Achievable, Realistic and Timed).

For example: I want to run a marathon by 31 December 2024.

Even though you want to get fit. Setting a goal of running a marathon on a certain date ensures that your goal is *specific*. It is *measurable* as a marathon is 26 miles.

However, is your goal *achievable*? Are you fit and can you run?

Is your goal *realistic*? Can you make the time to train and to run 26 miles? Can you ask a friend to train with you to keep you accountable?

This is *timed* and this is measured for you when you turn up for the run and you are given a time when you complete it.

To get you started

- Write one smart goal for today.
- Write one smart goal for tomorrow.

Then plan your goals for the short, medium and long term.

Short Term

- Write smart goal number 1 for the short term (next 12 months).

- Write smart goal number 2 for the short term.

Medium Term

- Write smart goal number 1 for the medium term (next 2-5 years).

- Write smart goal number 2 for the medium term.

Long Term

- Write smart goal number 1 for the long term (next 5-10 years).

- Write smart goal number 2 for the long term.

Make your plan and break it down into small steps. This may seem overwhelming but when you start writing it down, you switch to your logical brain as your brain thinks this is now going to happen.

You might like to give yourself a lot of time for your plans to percolate in your head or you might, like me, want everything yesterday. Well, you can't have that, but you can have the next best thing and you can start making your plan tonight, after you have finished reading some of this book.

You also need to learn to prioritise YOUR life to form new habits and to keep on going. You will without doubt go back from time to time to your old habit, like tidying the bathroom before you put your trainers on, or putting away the dishes before you run out the door.

However, if you can identify this habit and you find yourself going off plan, recognise it, stop, think and focus on what you need to do, to get what you want in your life.

Be kind to yourself as no-one is perfect, but you are getting yourself on track step by step and that is all good.

If you need further help on what direction you need to take, or you would find the most fun or fulfilling, it may help to go back in time to revisit what gave you the most happiness and fulfilment and re-engage with your younger self.

We can never go back and be that person again, but we can revisit her to find out what we loved in those times and perhaps repeat them to find our true selves again.

In the next chapter, let's look at how we can develop our personal power.

Ideas to Action

(1) How have other people described you?

(2) How would you describe yourself now?

(3) What would you like your identity to be?

(4) How would you describe the person you want to be?

(5) How can you move towards that?

(6) What would you advise a friend to do?

(7) What can you do to help yourself?

(8) What don't you want?

(9) If not now, when are you going to do it?

(10) Will you regret NOT doing it on your death bed?

Actions to Empower

Make a list of your key achievements to date:-

① _____

_____

② _____

_____

③ _____

_____

④ _____

_____

⑤ _____

What would you like to achieve in the future?

⑥ _____

_____

⑦ _____

_____

⑧ _____

_____

⑨ _____

_____

⑩ _____

_____

CHAPTER 10

Personal Power

NOW THAT YOU HAVE reclaimed your identity, discovered your needs and rediscovered your core desires, let's develop them so you can live a more fulfilled life.

In this chapter I will explain how important it is to recognise and use your personal power as an individual human.

There is a certain power in being your true authentic self. No-one else can be you. If you can understand this, then you are free to speak your truth.

The chances are that when you are brave enough to share your personal journey, you will also attract and inspire other people to use their power and speak their truth instead of struggling alone.

In the US in the 1960s, Betty Friedan studied American housewives and their unhappiness despite living in wealthy and comfortable homes and detailed her findings in her outstanding book, 'The Feminine Mystique'*(1921)*.

Betty Friedan states, "Historically, women have been socialised to believe that using their personal power, their voices, their achievements and having their own opinions, dreams and aspirations was less feminine. They were seen as somehow more selfish and less attractive to the opposite sex and had less attractive traits in society as a whole."

'The Feminine Mystique' is defined as an idealised version of housewives that women have tried to conform to. Despite their own individual lack of fulfilment, it explains that in post-World War II United States society, women were encouraged to be mothers and housewives and only mothers and housewives, with the home being defined as their domain and the world outside the home as the domain of men.

This thinking, hammered in via advertising, TV programmes, social structures, partners, mothers and fathers, conspired to give false promises that life for a woman (caged and constricted) in the home, was the ultimate fulfilment of a woman's purpose in society and for humankind.

This scenario was then re-enacted by women time and time again, as society told them they had to leave their jobs upon marriage to look after the home.

It must have been particularly difficult for women to return to the constraints that post war society placed on them after solving codes, making ammunition and being active in the war.

They had been useful in the exterior world, developed their intellectual abilities and ultimately contributed to breaking codes which stopped Hitler winning the war over the UK and so protected their country.

Yet when the men came back from war and needed jobs, half the humans had to return to an interior world as housewives.

The repercussions of the creation of the 'perfect family life', where woman is the housekeeper, mother, cook, events organiser, administrator, shopper, maintenance manager etc, are still being seen and felt by women today.

They kept family lives harmonious and felt the full pressure of society. They basically had to martyr themselves for the greater good of their family, at the cost of their own identity, colleagues, peers, friends, dreams, ambitions, happiness, intellectual stimulation, creativity and independent lives.

Friedan declared that women were also kept in a state of immaturity as they were encouraged to marry young and were expected to give up their own individual identity; jobs, support networks, education, personal fulfilment and intellectual stimulation.

However, the pressure to conform to these ideals, left women drinking alone in their homes, seeking help from therapists and sometimes being suicidal. They believed that there was something wrong with them, when in fact they were living a half-life, living a life through their husband's job or their children's lives.

Ultimately this was unfulfilling for women and stunted their intellectual development. Tasks such as perfecting the ironing, cooking a meal for the family or keeping the house clean and tidy were being sold as the ultimate fulfilment of a woman in society. This mantra was so heavily ingrained that thousands of women left school without any qualifications to marry young and 'settle down'.

Analysing this phrase, 'down' is the operative word here. The reality was that this living in a box lifestyle was repetitive and low intellect work. This would be the cause of so much frustration and individual under-achievement that many intellectual women were literally frustrated and sometimes bored to death by suicide.

Women today still live with this ideal of femininity and womanhood, which still resonates and permeates our world from the 1940s to the present day, over 80 years later.

Living a 'half-life' may appear to be a successful life on the surface. However, as an individual human being we all have the need to self-actualise, according to Maslow's Hierarchy of Needs - Maslow, Abraham: 'A Theory of Human Motivation' Psychological Motivation (1943).

Maslow's Hierarchy of Needs

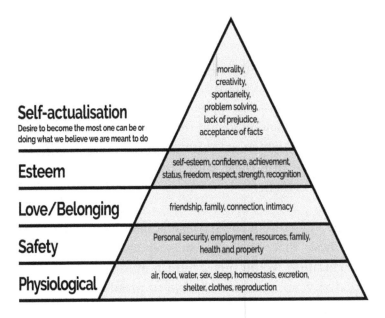

You will see from the diagram above, that Maslow said that ALL humans have needs which start with physical needs (at the bottom of the triangle such as air, food, water, shelter, sleep, clothing and to reproduce).

After those needs are met, humans then move up to the next step of the triangle and seek safety needs such as security, employment, resources, health and property. When women stayed at home and men went out to work, these needs were being secured by the men and enjoyed by both parties, but we all know that there is deep fulfilment in achieving for oneself.

Next, humans have needs for friendship, intimacy, a family and community. These are mostly organised by the female in the household but enjoyed by both partners.

Upwards of that, humans need to feed their esteem by gaining respect, status, recognition, strength and freedom. This is clearly the journey that the man of the household would enjoy, in the exterior world and then in his home, which was often seen as a reason why he didn't have to engage with tasks in the home, as his 'status' was higher.

At the very top of the triangle is the desire to become the best that one can be, which is called self-actualisation. To do this, a human must enjoy morality, creativity, spontaneity, be able to problem solve, lack prejudice and accept facts.

All humans need to grow as people, by realising their full potential and we get to this stage by intellectual and creative endeavours. Humans seek to fulfil all their needs on the triangle by working upwards but not always in a direct line because of the unpredictability of life.

It is hard to respect yourself when you are on the floor cleaning it and it is very difficult to be spontaneous and get to the top of the triangle (to achieve your true potential as a human), when you are carrying a 10lb baby or whilst you are breast feeding and up to your ears in dirty nappies. And when the world conspires to pressure you into believing everyone else's needs are more important than your own, it is nearly impossible.

Therefore, I believe as women we are #Womanhooded.

Fortunately, times are changing but not soon enough.

However, I believe if you plan out your life and refer to it (in words or pictures) you can still aim to reach the top of the pyramid and gain deep fulfilment.

Don't forget you will need to keep your focus and ask for help, in order to self-actualise. Asking for help is not a weakness, it's being assertive. You cannot do everything, you are a human being, not a robot and you will need to look after yourself with regular rest, exercise, good nutritious food and lots of water. Think of yourself as a machine that needs oil, fuel or electricity, a valet, treating well, regular maintenance, the best fuel and if you get over-used and overheated, you will simply burn out.

Life is so much easier with the help of a supportive family and/or partner or you can get together with other supportive women and support each other depending on what works for you, or possibly do both.

Make sure you also have the tools you need, be it self-care, sellotape, post-its, notepads, coloured pens or highlighters and make it fun.

Use Your Voice

Communication skills have been identified as key skills for the future and it is essential that women learn to speak up and present themselves so that they can be seen and heard. We each have a unique experience of the world and a way of thinking.

If, like me, you have lots of good ideas, you need to claim them to make the point that it was you who had the idea when people use it. Sarah Luisa Santos coined a phrase for this phenomenon recently.

"Bropriating (bro + appropriating) to refer to when a man appropriates an idea that a woman came up with and acts as if it were his, taking the credit for himself." (*Feminist Words New Vocabulary to Empower Yourself in Babbel online (4 March 2020)*).

I would say that both successful men and women do this to get noticed and up the career ladder, in my experience. However, the truth is, if someone uses your idea you need to own it and ensure you get credit for it.

I've also had managers of both genders who aimed to keep their employees low and not tell them how good they were, so that they were kept in their place and didn't ask for a pay rise!

In the UK, people are typically reserved, but this British reserve does not help our cause. If you are not confident at communicating what you want in your relationships or your work life, then you will be at a disadvantage.

People are not mind readers, so the sooner you learn to ask for what you want, the sooner you will get it, so please don't sit around frustrated or angry because people are not doing what you think they should.

If your partner, child or family needs direction from you, then simply tell them you would like a chat and discuss your problem or ask for their help. Chances are they will be happy too.

If there is any form of criticism involved, I find it is very helpful to use the 'appraisal sandwich'. This praises a behaviour such as, "I really appreciate you feeding the cat, but I am short of time tomorrow, could you please buy more cat food, as this would be really helpful."

In work, you can use this same method with your colleagues.

What if you demand more respect for 'your best friend' (yourself). You see that girl working so hard, talented, overlooked and going unseen. She is you and you are her. Start using your voice more in meetings, putting your hand up and volunteering for extra tasks such as presenting to the team.

You will stand out and you will grow in confidence as you learn and push yourself out of your comfort zone. If you feel scared doing a new task, it means that you are developing.

Speak your Truth

I am in awe of people who speak about their past, especially when it has been difficult. I think they are so courageous.

You can learn a lot from your past and by speaking your truth on a public platform, such as a book or a video on social media. You can also gather people around you who have similar experiences, who can empathise with you, know how you feel and will support you.

Women do better when they are in a group. We are hard wired to seek out groups as this has enabled our survival.

It is useful to remember your own past, so you don't make the same mistakes but learn from it and improve. We should appreciate the present as it is truly all that we have, but hopefully you are on the way to being empowered to design your own future.

Ask for it

Once you start doing this, you might get a shock, you might get respect, you might get agreement and you might be surprised. Women asking for what they want is empowering for women, it is also empowering for men. They know what you are thinking, they know what you want clearly (without trying to work it out themselves) so it's a win-win situation.

Start today or start tonight but think about what you want and then think about how you are going to ask for it. If you are not used to asking for what you want, you might need to practice it out loud first.

Take one hour to yourself. Not thinking about your partner, the kids, the house, or your job. Think about who you are, who you want to be and what you need to do to be it.

Be Confident

I hope these tips and actions help to improve your confidence and get what you want.

This is easier said than done, but if you work on your skills and talents, on what you enjoy and what you are naturally good at, then this will give you more confidence and reassurance.

Don't say 'Just'!

'Just' is another word that women routinely use.

When did you last hear someone say, "Can I just get past?" Or "Can I just ask you something?" Was it a man? Was it a woman?

Saying 'just' in this context

- disempowers us;
- diminishes our agency (which is your capacity to influence your own thoughts and behaviour); and
- diminishes what YOU have done, so you undermine your own actions and lose faith in yourself.

By diminishing your agency, you are taking away your own sense of control that you feel in your life and your capacity to influence your own thoughts and behaviour.

If you diminish what you do yourself, then you won't get proper credit for your actions and can't leverage them to show your contributions.

Why are you adding the word 'just' into your sentences? "Can I just speak to you for a minute?" Why not say, "Can I speak to you for a minute?" If you say 'just' before a sentence it also cues the other person to behave in a certain way and not take you seriously.

So next time you use the word "just", think, is it "just you" or is it YOU. You are as important as the next person in the queue, in the relationship or in society. We are all important, so don't 'just' ask. Ask and cue your audience to listen and respond with the appropriate respect.

Apologies

There is power in the words you use and don't use.

This past year I have noticed that a lot of women use the word 'sorry' like confetti, sprinkling it everywhere in abundance, but what are they apologising for? Their existence? It seems like it. Do you do this?

I used to do this too usually to be polite, but now that I have recognised this, I stop myself. I reframe my words. For example, I used to say "sorry about that" or use "sorry" at the start of a text message. Now I ask myself, have I done anything wrong? If not, I rewrite my sentence for example.

"Sorry for taking ages to reply...". I now say "How are you? I'd love to see you so would you like to meet up or are you free for a phone call?" Chances are your friends are busy too and are delighted to hear from you. What's to be sorry for?

I am not sure where or why I started it, but I have noticed that by saying sorry when not necessary, it again disempowers us, diminishes our personal power and gives people an excuse to blame us when it's not our fault.

Of course, you can and should say it if you happen to tread on someone's foot or you have hurt their feelings in some way, but saying "sorry, can I?" doesn't help anyone. This can make the other person feel artificially important and cue them to talk down to you or treat you with less respect from your lowly, apologetic stance.

Say it if you have genuinely done something wrong and mean it but otherwise, stop.

Once you have noticed this pattern of behaviour, you can change it and go on to be the agent of your own destiny.

Ask yourself:

- When did you last say sorry for something?
- How did the other person react?
- How did it make you feel?
- Do you say it often?
- How will you phrase your next text message?

SMART Planning

Now that you have found your voice and decided what you want to do, write it down, no matter how far-fetched. Then write down each steps towards reaching your goal.

Make it specific, date it and give yourself a big tick next to it when you have completed each step.

Celebrate what you have done so far and then pat yourself on the arm which sends a positive message to your brain too. Then move on to the next step, little by little you are moving towards your goal.

Make your goals SMART, Specific, Measured, Achievable, Realistic and Timed.

For example, I will write 1000 words of my blog by .... (insert date).

Once you have achieved your own personal goals, you could scale up to have a mission for the wider world.

I guarantee that you will feel more empowered, stronger, bolder and you will get more out of life, yourself, your friends, your employers and your family.

These are some of the most prevalent problems in the present day. Could you help solve them?

War - for power, for land, for status. The cost is that human lives are lost and families destroyed. Can you take even a small step to stop this from happening?

I don't want any more wars and I hope you don't either. It seems like the world is becoming more war torn and not developing strategies at a higher level for world peace.

As I write, Ukraine is under siege from Russia and now Israel and Hamas are at war over Gaza which threatens to be long lasting.

Join a march, set up a march even? Take a role in local politics, so that you start to represent ordinary people, to prevent war and suffering.

Plastic pollutants - fish and sea life are being destroyed by the selfishness of humans. Coral is dying and this is making a massive impact on the ocean. Research all the facts about how humans are killing sea life and the impact this could have on the planet.

Take steps to stop using plastic, tell all your friends and family or join a litter picking group to do your bit. Or think of a bigger, better idea for the re-use of plastic.

When travelling recently, I was shocked to find so much litter and plastic bottles about to go into the water system in Morocco. Dozens of plastic drinks bottles were thrown near a beautiful natural waterfall by thoughtless tourists.

I made it my mission to collect them using a plastic bag which was lodged in a bush and before we knew it, my friend Chelli Hardy and I had collected four bags and put them in a bin. If you start off, then others will follow.

A decade before that, on a small island in Greece, we took a boat trip to a beautiful island which was littered with drinks cans and plastic bottles. The man whose livelihood was at risk if this continued but it was lost on him so I took two bags of bottles back to the hotel.

My family thought I was mad, but I didn't care. It's our beautiful world, it is up to us to look after it.

Don't be part of the problem and always take your litter home with you.

Female Empowerment - women still do not have equity in the workforce, in the household and in their relationships. Think about what you are role modelling to your daughters and sons for the next generation?

You could cheerlead and support other women, highlight the differences between genders, put questions to those in power, inspire or mentor younger women.

If you act with agency (which is being in control of your own life) this will inspire them, after all, as the saying goes, you have to "see one to be one!"

Now that you are empowered to use your voice, words and actions, let's look at your Purchasing Power.

Ideas to Action

(1) When did you last use your voice to get what you wanted?

(2) How did it feel?

(3) Where could you use your voice more?

(4) What would you like to do to reach your potential?

(5) How would it feel?

(6) What would other people think?

(7) Does it even matter?

(8) Is it a good role model for your children?

(9) What might happen if you spoke your truth?

(10) Why don't you speak your truth?

Actions to Empower

(1) Do one thing to improve your self-esteem.
Say something positive about yourself out loud to a friend or family member.

(2) If you have a hang up (we all do) do one positive step to improve it.

(3) What are you most proud of achieving so far in your life?

(4) Assign yourself one creative mission this week.

(5) Have one spontaneous adventure this week.

(6) Solve a problem you have been avoiding by the end of this week.

(7) Identify a prejudice you have.
Talk about it and try to overcome it, so you don't repeat it.

(8) Read the news about women's equality.
Accept the facts and make a plan to improve it.

(9) Say a positive affirmation to yourself, such as "I am brilliant at planning events."

(10) Pat yourself on the arm while you say it out loud, for positive reinforcement.

CHAPTER 11

Purchasing Power

MANY OF THE DECISIONS you make are based on how much money and power you do or don't have. Do you buy Balenciaga, bargain basement brands or most likely something in between?

In this chapter I aim to show you how much purchasing power women have today. If you have the money, you have the choice. It's that simple.

Having money also has health benefits for you and your family. Cheap food typically has less nutrients and more chemicals than a more expensive organic version that will be free from artificial ingredients such as colours, preservatives and E-numbers.

When I was a student, all I could afford was chips and so my weight increased and I believe if I had carried on past the three-year course, my health would have suffered. Can you imagine what the health implications of long-term poverty are for a woman trying to feed her family?

So why do we so often feel uneasy when talking about what we earn and how much more that extra responsibility or a specific set of skills can earn us?

In 2023, it's still uncomfortable and a social taboo across the social classes to ask that question and in some parts of the UK it is considered rude and intrusive.

If you can't ask the questions, you can't get the answers and therefore you can't take action to improve your own finances and life chances.

I was brought up with the saying that "children should be seen and not heard". Then later as a school child was told, "don't be rude" when asking 'intrusive' questions such as, "what job do you do?"

Looking back on this conditioning, it was key to me finding out about future jobs I could work towards, finding a role model and raising my expectations of my future self as well. This taboo has been with me all my life as I have always felt that I couldn't ask that question of any of the adults I spent time with. Do you feel like this too?

Later, I would never dream of probing further to ask any family or friends how much they earned, what perks they had in their job such as company car, commission, bonuses or discounts. As a woman, being unable to discuss money with male colleagues has the consequence that you then can't increase your salary and benefits to be in line with any man you know.

Why? Because in our capitalist society, your inherent 'value' as a person is linked to how much you earn, which is linked to what opportunities you are given, what life chances you take, what job you do, where you holiday, what car you drive and what brands you wear.

However, in order to be happy, you also need a balance, which is unfortunately invisible to others. Only YOU know how happy you are, as it is not measured and can vary by the minute. In general, you need enough stress to keep you stimulated, but not too much that you feel overworked and anxious. This will then have a negative impact on your health and well-being and that of your family so needs to be sorted out.

It's painful to earn a large salary if you are not happy in your own mind and body.

What is the price you would accept, before responsibilities of bills, electricity, gas, petrol, children, mortgage, rent or car loans, to do the job you love and pay for the lifestyle you want?

Do you work to live, or live to work? That is the question to ask yourself, because so many of us are working to survive and pay bills. I believe that being unfulfilled and unhappy can shorten our lives as much as a poor diet.

Earning Money

Women traditionally earn less than men because in the past men were expected to support their whole family, while women were expected to work in the home once they were married.

However, this traditional set up has not caught up with the modern world, where women are sometimes the only wage earner in a household and may have to work two jobs to keep themselves out of debt. Therefore, this isn't fair or equal.

This is still the same world over, so trailblazing women in Iceland including Prime Minister Katrin Jakobsdottir, went on strike, at work and in the home, to protest against the gender pay gap.[4]

Don't accept this in your own working life in the UK. Find out what the men who do the same job as you are earning and if you are not earning the same, speak to your manager so that they can change it and get it backdated. The law is on your side.

If you don't get equal wages, or it's happening too slowly and you feel like you are being fobbed off, go to your Union, bring it to their attention to deal with or even write to your local newspaper who can highlight it and champion your cause. If your company finds out about

---

[4] *Iceland's PM strikes over gender pay gap - BBC.co.uk, Tuesday, 24 October 2023*

your plans, they will soon speed up their process, believe me!

You may need to reconsider your career, so ask yourself, what do you love about your job or what would your dream job be?

If it doesn't pay you enough money to support the lifestyle you need or want, you need to make more money.

Women generally undervalue their skills and experience and it has been well documented that when applying for a job, men will apply if they have most of the key skills, but women will only apply if they have all the skills required. In reality, if you have most of the required skills and the company likes you, they will develop you, so be positive.

You need to have a plan and take positive steps towards your goals, one by one. If you want a pay rise you need to be assertive, if you want a promotion, you need to be assertive.

Make time to look at your options and take steps towards doing a better paid job. For example, research what qualifications you need for this job online, apply for the role, or ask advice via acquaintances or on LinkedIn. Ask whether you could shadow them or could they mentor you to get a similar job?

The Gender Pay Gap

There is a growing realisation that women are penalised for having a womb. Why aren't penises penalised?

In truth, the fact that women have wombs and can incubate a human being is incredible.

To be able to feed, water, keep warm, grow and protect a baby is something that only females in the animal and human world can do (except for sea horses) and this should form our USP (unique selling point) and increase our value.

Does this happen in reality?

There are a limited number of humans who have the ability to spend 40 weeks doing this valuable work because without women, the whole human race would die out.

We need to know this, own it and know our worth. Then perhaps men would too.

However, our life-giving wombs are being weaponised against us. This is how.

If you look at the female lifecycle and the fact that most women will go on to have children, it will look like this; from birth, to childhood, to being a teenager, to adulthood, to motherhood and looking after parents, to being an empty nester, to retirement and eventually you die, on average around 85 years old.

Research shows that 81% of caregivers are female and the average woman gives 20 hours per week of unpaid care to parents. Therefore, the pressure is on women and may further impact their working hours and quality of life as many choose to leave their job, reduce their hours or take early retirement.

One result of these caregiving responsibilities is that studies have shown that women have on average £123,000 less than a man upon retirement.[5]

Added to this "Women are behind in every area of personal finance, from the gender pay gap to the gender literacy gap, to the gender investment gap" *(Holly Holland and Laura Pomfret from Financielle.co.uk (2002).*[6]

They say that from an early age of 8 years old, girls receive on average 5% less pocket money than boys. Why do you think this is?

This discrepancy gets larger over the years when females begin working.[7]

The huge gap between female and male pay is slowly reducing from the near 10% in 2019. However, it is still

---

[5] *Source: ScottishWidows.co.uk, 2023*

[6] *https://www.financielle.co.uk/1650000000000-2/*

[7] *Source: Youth Economy Report, go henry.com*

the case that many men, in today's world still leave the home to earn the majority of the family income and take on most of the financial pressure.

Just look at the information below which is directly quoted from the Office of National Statistics' website (November 2022).

"The gender pay gap has been declining slowly over time. Over the last decade it has fallen by approximately a quarter for both full-time employees and all employees. In 2022, the gap among full-time employees increased to 8.3%, up from 7.7% in 2021. This is still below the gap of 9.0% before the coronavirus pandemic in 2019, which affected the weakest and poorest in society the most. Estimates for 2020 and 2021 are subject to more uncertainty than usual, therefore we recommend looking at the longer-term trend. Among all employees, the gender pay gap decreased to 14.9%, from 15.1% in 2021, but is still below the levels seen in 2019 (17.4%).

The gender pay gap for part-time employees also reduced from negative 3.0% to negative 2.8%. The upward trend in the part-time gender pay gap seen since 2015 is continuing.

The gender pay gap is higher for all employees than it is for full-time employees or part-time employees. This is because women fill more part-time jobs, which in comparison with full-time jobs have lower hourly median pay".

Lockdown is said to have further impacted more women than men.

As you can see, it is even worse for women if they work part-time. In my experience and that of my friends, finding a part-time job which can be done at the same time as school hours (including travel there and back) is very hard to find.

My friend, Lisa Payne identified a need for part-time hours and tried to set up a recruitment company that focused on a parent pool of dedicated, skilled, experienced workers. The problem was that there was a huge pool of parents looking for part-time roles, but it was difficult to find employers who valued these qualities, therefore few companies to recruit for. She simply could not balance the two and the demand from the employers took precedence as they had the spending power. This is just one example of how women and families continue to be disadvantaged.

When women become mothers, this is detrimental to their future earnings in comparison with fathers. Whilst on maternity leave, women miss pension contributions, tax relief, promotional opportunities and the growth potential from those investments over time.

Add to this that women often return part-time due to the high cost of childcare in the UK which further decreases their earning potential and lessens their contributions towards their pension pot for their future.

Pensions

It was International Women's Day recently and as I write; Scottish Widow's Insurance has shone a light on how much less women's pensions are in comparison with men's. They have collective figures and can see the unfairness and injustice of this when in reality we are all working hard. Males outside the home and females now outside and inside the home.

If you could start with one thing, take a deep breath (like you would in labour and breathe through the pain!) and use your voice. Start talking about this unfairness and any other, with your friends and with your family, make a list and take action to support change, step by step.

I don't know about you, but I personally find talking about finances difficult, but it is a short-term pain you need to go through to benefit in the long term. As the hugely intuitive Glennon Doyle said "we can do hard things!"

The law is clear for married women who share pension rights with their spouses, but if you are unmarried and have taken on these child-caring and/or parent-caring duties, then you need to find out where you stand. Do you benefit from your partner's pension or are you left in a weaker position? The caring duties are primarily left to women, so why not the pension too?

You should have a conversation with your partner if you are presumed to be taking on the caring responsibilities of children or parents and you should increase your pension contributions to make up for the time out and share caring responsibilities equally.

It is also beneficial to you and your children for you to be financially savvy, so if you cannot do it for you, do it for your children.

Saving Money

Get into the habit of saving 20% of your earnings and put it into a high interest bank or building society account. You will get used to spending what is left and won't notice the difference after a while, but all the time will be saving up for your future, for further education, for a car, for a house or for travelling the world.

Having money gives you more choices in life and worse still, having little money limits your choices. It also takes away the potential worry of getting into debt and having to pay spiralling interest rates or bank charges for being overdrawn.

Investing Money

Be part of the upward spiral in your finances, not the downward spiral into debt. Interest rates are cumulative, which means that for each year you save, your interest will increase as your savings increase.

Make sure you get the best rate by comparing interest rates online when you open your bank and/or savings account and make a diary note on your calendar to check each year that you are getting the best rate. If not, switch to the highest rate as over time this will make a big difference.

Based on simple figures of £100 and an interest rate of 4% you could save the following:

Year 1 for each £100 you save = £104.00
Year 2 then the next year (4% of £104.00) = £108.16
Year 3 you will gain (4% of 108.16) = £112.50
Year 4 (4% of 112.50) = £117.00
Year 5 (4% of 117.00) = £121.60

This example shows the cumulative effect, assuming the interest rate stays the same and you don't add more savings, for simplicity. This interest rate will go up or down based on the banks and the state of the economy.

Conversely, if you take out a loan, or go into an overdraft of £100, you will have to pay the loan interest rate and perhaps a penalty too. Therefore, from an initial loan of £100 and an interest rate of 10%, your debt will increase unless you pay it off quickly.

£100 loan = £110.00 debt
Year 2 = £121.00
Year 3 = £133.10
Year 4 = £146.41
Year 5 = £161.00

Most interest rates on loans are far more than this and adverts for loans often show interest rates of 46%. Legally they must show the rate which they put as APR (Annual Percentage Rate), but unless you know what that means, it confuses the audience even further, thus maximising the company's profits.

I saw this loan company advertised on TV recently with an APR of 149%. This should not be legal and preys on the desperate or financially uneducated, which is partly why they have had to take out a loan in the first place. It is pure greed.

Below is an example of how this works: APR 46% loan of £100:

Year 1 = £146.00 owed
Year 2 = £213.16 owed
Year 3 = £311.21 owed
Year 4 = £454.36 owed
Year 5 =£ 663.37 owed

This is if the interest rate stays the same and doesn't increase further.

Therefore, you can see how this debt can very easily spiral out of control. My advice is don't do it, don't spend the money you do not have, save up first, or buy something on Facebook marketplace (and save the planet in the meantime). You could also sell what you don't use or swap it with a friend or relative. You could go to a charity shop and buy something unique and cheaper too. Or be creative and make something of your own or update something you already own. You can easily add a tassel or a badge to a jacket from a haberdashery shop or buy it online or change the buttons at a fraction of the cost to you and the planet.

Risk

If an investment seems too good to be true, then it is TOO GOOD TO BE TRUE and is likely to be a scam. BEWARE.
Also, only bet on what you can afford to lose.

I learnt this recently when I put a bet on two horses at The Grand National at Aintree, Liverpool. I set up an app which took me 2 minutes and set up a £50 limit. I got the betting bug and couldn't put a second bet on the first betting app, so I quickly and easily set up a second app with another £50 limit.

So, I lost £50 on the first app and £50 on the second app in literally 6 minutes. The barriers to not betting don't go far enough and it is very easy to see how gambling can spiral out of control.

Las Vegas residents don't pay taxes because the gamblers who go there lose such vast sums of money it pays for the whole city.

Don't be a fool and be SMART with your money.

Women have a lot of pressure on them to look good as I've said before and to look different by perhaps changing their makeup, hairstyle, hair colour, clothes, shoes, or bag so it's important that you don't get pressured into spending lots of money on items that lose value overnight, rather than investing your money into long term goals.

Support

It might be useful to get a couple of friends involved so that you can celebrate your wins together, which is important to keep you motivated and happy. Once people know your mindset, then you will attract other thrifty friends and can swap money saving tips together. It will feel boring or alien at first, but once you see the results, you will be richer and get a buzz out of it. Trust me.

Recently there has been some media coverage to show that women pay more for living as they need to buy certain products like sanitary products and have little choice. The government has gone a little way towards understanding this and has taken the tax off these products, but it could go further and make them free.

Life does not have to be expensive to be fun. Your kids and partner mostly need quality time and your full attention to keep them happy.

The next chapter will demonstrate how you are manipulated into spending a lot of your precious time on products that you don't need, when you could be spending more time developing your skills, spending quality time with your family or reaching your potential.

Ideas to Action

(1) Think about a possible career change if yours is not flexible enough or you're not earning enough.

(2) Think about how you could earn more.

(3) Have a money mindset so you know how much you have to spend each week and don't go over it.

(4) Do some research on well-paid jobs.

(5) Look at what qualifications and experience you would need to do them.

(6) Think about what you would like to have or do in the future and plan for it now.

(7) Think about how you could invest more so you have a good financial future.

(8) Talk about pensions with female friends so they too are aware and plan for their future.

(9) Talk about the female lifecycle and swap tips on how you can make it easier for each other.

(10) Talk about how you would like to spend your retirement and how much money you would need for it.

Actions to Empower

1. Ask for a pay rise. Write a list of what you have achieved at work, what responsibilities you have taken on and what skills and qualifications you have gained since your last pay award. Research other roles in the same field to prove what the current rate is. (Having the research in number format provides vital information to back up your request).

2. Arrange a direct debit to put 10-20% of your take home pay into a high interest bank or building society account the day after you are paid so that you aren't tempted to spend it.

3. Find out what your pension is worth now and increase your contributions by direct debit and/or your HR department. (If you work for a company, your employers generally match your contribution, so by putting in more, you gain more).

4. Employ a financial advisor as they will save you money in the long term. Ask them how your pension could be increased to give you the lifestyle you want at 55/60/65/68/70 or whatever age you plan to retire.

5. When you go to the till in a shop, be nice to the assistant, give them a smile and make a comment on their day. Ask them if they offer a discount for paying cash or have any other discounts?

6. Create a budget. This will help you stay focused and more likely to hit it.

7. Review your budget weekly.

8. Review your budget monthly.

9. Review your budget yearly to keep on track

10. Pat yourself on the arm for positive reinforcement while you tell yourself what a big step you have taken towards your family finances.

CHAPTER 12

The Beauty and Fashion Industry

AS WOMEN WE ARE 'taught' that our value will decrease over time as our youthful looks fade and our body gets older. However, what about all the experience, skills and personal qualities we have gained over our lifetime?

It seems that society is obsessed with women 'looking great', but what is our ultimate aim? If we do look 'perfect', what then? Will we feel fully satisfied or underwhelmed? I don't know, I've never been there. Have you?

We are bombarded 24/7 with beautifying products for hair, clothes, makeup, skincare and fitness - on Facebook, on Instagram, on TikTok, on X, on YouTube, on TV, in magazines, in newspapers and online.

How many hours a week do you spend scrolling through social media, flicking through TV channels, all the time taking in conscious and subconscious messages such as "You have this problem, here's the solution, buy this". Buy, buy, buy!

Where does this constant onslaught want you to go? To the till that's where, so that you can spend your hard-earned cash on the never-ending quest to be perfect. And so, you put it in the basket and end up yet another basket case!

Now I am not against looking good and feeling great, after all if you look after yourself on the outside, it goes hand in hand with feeling great on the inside.

However, we women have more depth and beneath the surface veneer we have thoughts, feelings, needs, aspirations and emotions. Don't get me wrong, there's joy in buying a new lipstick or pair of shoes, but there is also a deeper, more productive and longer lasting joy in learning a new skill or being creative.

Women are complex, intelligent humans, with deeper needs and desires, but social expectations focus on a thin veneer that has been identified as "the male gaze", Wikipedia (2023) which is the act of depicting women and the world in media and literature from a masculine, heterosexual perspective. It shows how women are represented as objects to be looked at for the pleasure of heterosexual male viewers. In the wider world this means they are further viewed as objects.

However, true human happiness comes with developing your deeper layers, so it's crucial to keep evolving your individual personality, passions, education and identity with humour, courage, determination, drive and honesty, in order to fulfil your potential and feel satisfied.

We have more choice than ever and can buy products that have an ethical element, such as choosing pre-loved clothes or longer lasting items, instead of fast fashion (which is often tipped into landfill sites at the end of the season).

Not only are women the largest section of the population, but we are also responsible for the most spend.

"By 2028, women will own 75% of the discretionary spend, making them the world's greatest influencers. Yet, around the world, women are shouldering more of the household burdens, feeling less financially secure and are still facing serious barriers when it comes to equality" - *Nielsen.com 2022*

We are gaining more control of the spending in the economy and making the daily decisions on what to buy and who to buy from.

Therefore, I believe we also have a moral responsibility (at the top of Maslow's triangle) to take account of the world now and in the future, using our experience and values, we have the power of choice.

We can choose to buy products that do not harm animals as started by founder Dame Anita Lucia Roddick DBE at The Body Shop in 1976. She wanted to produce cosmetics without harming animals and support females in third world countries and reduce plastic consumption, so became a huge force for good which was revolutionary at the time.

"I think all business practices would improve immeasurably if they were guided by feminine' principles"
- Dame Anita Roddick

Caring about the future of the planet has led to a vast shift in our purchasing habits and choosing products that are recyclable, as we all try to reduce the huge environmental impact of plastic bottles cluttering the oceans.

You can use this power positively to make educated choices and if we all make these beneficial choices, then the rest of the beauty industry will have to adapt if they wish to survive.

In the past, the Customer was King, now the customer is Queen.

Your Body

We are bombarded with images of perfection and now it's more than doubled since the advent of social media.

It's hard to absorb the fact that people are often filtered and their less than perfect body parts are edited to present the best image or brand - even Kim Kardashian does this!

Life is too short to sit at home worrying that you are too fat or too thin, too much or not enough.

So if you don't like something about your face or body, these days you can choose to have it fixed, be it your brows or your breasts.

It's your body so your choice and if you need some tweaks to feel confident, then so be it, but it is only a part of your identity, not your whole being. If making a change enables you to achieve more, be more confident and be happy in your life, then why not?

Clothes Shopping

In the UK, shopping became a national obsession when shops opened on Sundays.

And it's very easy to get caught in a trap of spend, spend, spend whether you need something or not.

If you do seem to spend a lot of time buying stuff, ask yourself:

a) Do I need it?
b) Can I afford it?

Added to this, fashion buying is the second biggest pollutant of the world as most surplus or unsold big brand, high fashion clothes are sent away to a third world country and thrown into a landfill.

This is because they don't want to sell their items cheaply, as it will depreciate their brand value. Don't be a part of driving this demand for fast fashion and limit your new purchases. Instead, you could buy quality or pre-loved pieces, that won't go in and out of fashion and then end up on the tip.

You can still look great in a more classic style and less repeat purchases will leave you with headspace and energy, so you can use your time for something more productive.

I got out of the habit of shopping every Saturday when I had kids, as I would look around for an hour or two, then try on clothes, get hot, stressed and sometimes stuck with a too tight top on my shoulders with my arms held high, like in a truss. Then the baby would wake up, get bored, start crying and the sound drilled into my brain, so I had to get changed and to the till quick and by then the baby would ALWAYS be screaming in the queue.

I got more and more stressed and got more and more dirty looks from other people who were getting stressed out too. I would either pay for the goods and run out of the shops with tears in my eyes or just leave the hard-found items in their basket and go home stressed, frustrated and exhausted. At the time, this was very painful, but the good news is that it literally put me off shopping for 10 years!

I look back now and think, why did I do that? Partly because I'd been trained from a young age to shop, shop and shop, which is a tough trap to escape from. I also didn't have the headspace to think what else I could do, as it's so much easier to repeat what you have always done.

However, once you've recognised you're in a trap, you can get yourself out of it. In hindsight, I should have arranged to have a coffee with friends more or invited them to mine and then arranged a day or night out, as 'quality' time without the kids.

If you are at this stage now, with young children demanding all your time and attention, then please do this at least once and let me know on Instagram what you can do instead.

The Customer Lifecycle

Having worked in marketing for many years, you learn you can market to different people at different ages and stages of their lives.

For example, you may have heard of DINKY (Dual Income No Kids Yet). This age group has a high disposable income and most of the money is spent on themselves.

Once you have one or more children, the majority of parents' income is spent on supporting their children, so marketing is spent on highlighting their children's needs to instigate a purchase.

At the other end of the human lifecycle, the term 'empty nesters' was coined for the time in life when the chicks have left the nest (children have left home). The parents then have a higher disposable income for their own fun again, including visiting restaurants, buying clothes or travelling abroad.

The Buying Process

A lot of money and research has been invested in identifying these life stages which in turn has meant that marketing is highly targeted towards individuals in what is called a Decision Making Unit (DMU) coined by Philip Kotler.

These individual roles occur singly or together in order to make a purchase:

1. **The Initiator** - this person identifies a need, for example you need an office chair so that you can work from home.

2. ***The Influencer*** (way before the social media influencers of today were even born!) - you mention what you want to a friend when you go out for a coffee and she says she has seen a great one on Instagram and she shows you the page where she saw it, it looks good and they do it in the colour you like too.

You then mention it to your Mum who says she has seen one on sale at the shops, you know she's good at getting good deals, so you take a trip to the shops and try it out. Word of mouth works!

3. ***The Gatekeeper*** - now you share the office with your partner, so you ask for their thoughts too. They say yes, it's nice but have you thought about one with a massage element as you both have bad backs.

4. ***The Decider*** - you look online at the shop your Mum has flagged up and see the chair with a heating and massage function and decide to upgrade your chair choice.

5. ***The Buyer*** - you notice it is 10% off your first order if you buy from their website, so you put in your card details and physically buy the chair online.

6. ***The User*** - when the chair arrives, it's what you both want and you both use it regularly when you work in the office. You've listened and upgraded and now both users are happy, you with a good deal and them with the extra massage.

As you can imagine, women play key roles in ultimately buying any given product for the home, their face or body, their partner, mother, father, friend, sister, brother, cousin, team, boss, son or daughter.

It is high time we claimed these roles and realise that in the vast majority of cases, as customers, we initiate, influence and ultimately buy so many products.

In the UK, Eleanor Mills, Founder of noon.org.uk, in collaboration with Accenture, found that in December 2022 women over 40 earned more money than those under 40 for the first time and named them 'Queenagers'. They are educated, affluent, open-minded and outspend millennials by 250%.

Queenagers (45-65s) are behind 90% of all household spending decisions. The over 50s control 47% of the UK's wealth. Adverts focus on the menopause, but in reality, this group routinely buys expensive items like holidays, leisure activities and cars. They have the two most valuable assets in terms of customer qualities, time and disposable income.

In the rest of the world, according to GirlPowerMarketing.com, "women control over $31.8 Trillion in worldwide spending. Of this they purchase 91% of new homes, 66% of personal computers, 92% of holidays, 65% of new cars, 89% of bank accounts and 93% of food."

Other fascinating facts include:-

- The average traveller is a 47-year-old female who wears a size 12 dress.
- 77% of women take a man along to car dealerships to prevent being taken advantage of!
- 84% of US women are the sole preparer of household meals, at least 5 times per week.

Women differ substantially from men in how they relate to investing. They don't want to hear about the growth or comparative performance of different funds; they want information about reaching their long-term goals, like putting a child through college as stated by *Vanguard Group's Asset Management Services Division.*

In the US, they make up more than half the population and control or influence 85% of consumer spending according to *Forbes (2019).*

The beauty and well-being industry is a multi-billion-pound industry. It is not going away. If you are a woman, I hope that you are making money from it, as well as supporting it.

I am not asking you to stop buying beauty products and looking after yourself (which is good for your mental and physical health).

However, make no mistake. YOU have the power to choose and influence what happens in the world. Now you recognise this power, I ask you to think about what you buy and choose carefully.

Buy and Bin Responsibly

As an incentive, Boots now offers advantage points if you bring five empty beauty products to their store. Maybelline provides beauty recycling bins to Tesco, Superdrug and Boots including eyeshadows, foundations, mascaras and lipsticks. Origins counters will also accept and separate old packaging.

Switch your single use wipes for washable face cloths, they were wise in the old days.

Electrical items can be taken to your local recycling centre or use Cloud Nine's recycling scheme. Go to their website and fill out a form to be sent a pre-paid label, which you then take with your electrical products to the Post Office, who will then send them to be refurbished or broken down into raw materials for re-use.

Cotton buds are now recyclable and can go on your compost tip as well as card and paper packaging, so they can go into the soil and help to grow new trees and plants.

Now that you see how much can be bought as an individual woman, we can broaden that to see how many decisions are subsequently made each day by each woman compared to an average man.

Ideas to Action

1. How could you be more ethical in your purchasing decisions?

2. Do you look at re-cycle logos on skin care and make up containers?

3. What could you do today to reduce plastic in your home?

4. What ethical brands could you use?

5. What can you put into your composter?

6. What brands do you use that are not animal friendly?

7. What brands do you use that are not environment friendly?

8. Can you collect old beauty containers and return them?

9. Have you got a recycling shop near you for refills?

10. Could you re-cycle more?

Actions to Empower

1. Buy less products and save yourself money.

2. Research and choose ethical products and brands before you buy anything.

3. Ensure you use products that do not harm animals. Are they PETA registered (People for the Ethical Treatment of Animals? A leaping bunny logo meets cruelty-free standards).

4. Use products that do not harm the environment and use less plastic, such as Too Faced uses recyclable card packaging. (A green or black logo of a triangle of arrows demonstrates a recyclable product).

5. Tell your friends and family what you do and why, so they can look out for the signs and buy ethically too.

6. Don't buy plastic bottles. Buy a drinks container you love and refill it daily, so you drink lots of water, which helps your body repair and hydrate.

7. Wherever you travel, take a plastic bag and do your bit for the earth. Collect any rubbish you see there and put it in a bin. Your children and grandchildren will thank you for it as thousands of fish, coral and sea creatures can't.

8. Get other people to help you pick up litter.

9. Give yourself positive self-talk, such as "I helped save the planet today."

10. Pat yourself on the arm while you say it out loud, for positive reinforcement.

CHAPTER 13

Women's Decision Making

BEING A WOMAN COMES with so many expectations of looking a certain way. A woman has to think of all the steps below, probably before she even has her morning drink or breakfast, before listening to the news or organising her children (if she has any).

In this chapter I'm going to break down the many steps that we take for granted, compared with the decisions a typical man has to make each and every day.

The way you present yourself says so much about you and your identity. Are you glamorous with time on your hands to have acrylic nails done every 3 weeks? Are you a practical lady who prefers clean short nails for your active lifestyle?

Are your shoes high, medium or flat? Do you wear them to impress someone in a meeting, feel more confident, gain some height, feel sexy?

Do you choose trainers to travel in, so you can walk or run for your train or bus?

Thankfully, fashion trends these days include women wearing trainers with dresses or suits. Therefore, from a practical point of view, they are not at a disadvantage if they need to run or walk a lot, they can be active and they can look stylish and feel confident.

This is a modern development which hails from New York, then London, where busy professional women put trainers on to get to work on busy public transport and then changed them at their desks to conform to company dress codes in the office.

Outside of work, women now wear trainers all the time, often with a flowery dress or long skirt for getting out and about.

To take it a step further, other practical decisions are to wear jeans and trousers instead of dresses or skirts. In the 1870s, women wore bustle skirts (to hide sanitary wear) and to show their wealth and status as they didn't have to do manual labour.

The women were purely decorative, as it was impossible to run, ride a bike, a horse, or do any other type of physical activity whilst wearing their skirts. They were weighed down and prevented from a lot of activities due to their clothes, which were impractical for anything other than sitting down in a carriage or going for a stroll.

In the 1910s, women's clothes became more tailored and we all know that post World War I, women wore the flapper dress which was more functional and flattened the bust line rather than accentuating it. The result was that women had more freedom and could dance!

In the 1930s Du Pont invented nylon, so women were able to wear Nylon dresses which were more practical to wash or dry and allowed for even greater movement.

During WWII, rationed fabrics meant that fashion was more utilitarian and formal such as the tailored suit jackets which men had worn, with square shoulders. They wore either pleated skirts that ended just below the knee and trousers became much more commonplace, as they replaced men in the workforce.

Thanks to the women's liberation movement, in the 1950s and 1960s, Capri trousers, invented by fashion designer Sonja de Lennart, were popularized by her and English couturier Bunny Roger. They were invented as normal trousers got wet when paddling on the beach, so trousers were shortened and tightened.

In 1960s and 70s, wearing a short skirt and showing your legs was seen as a signal to look at your legs (and unfortunately it would be a lot easier to lift up and put back down for an opportunist). Wearing a skirt could mean that you were unknowingly flashing your underwear to an unwelcome viewer. Longer skirts were therefore considered preferable and modest before the 1960s. Parents everywhere complained and feared the miniskirt as their girls rebelled.

In 1980s culture, the fashion was OTT with stupendous shoulder pads, huge hair and a surge of creative expression in makeup and cross dressing. People like Boy George represented for the first time the blurring of gender through fashion.

In the 1990s, the model, Kate Moss became an icon for looking cool with minimal makeup and wearing the simple, grunge style of clothes on her very slim frame.

It was unusual in 2015 for a girl in primary school to wear trousers. This meant that girls were disadvantaged at a young age, as it prevented them from doing some physical activities in the playground. They literally couldn't climb trees or do cartwheels, without flashing their knickers and for this they would be ridiculed and therefore less likely to do it. I do remember some girls wearing shorts as well as their skirts before the skort became available for school PE.

As late as 2018, I remember one daughter saying to another, if she wore trousers for her school uniform she would stand out as different and be bullied. So social pressures still prevailed. When you think about it, my daughter's preference was purely practical. She wanted to run, she wanted to play football, climb trees and run with her friends and she couldn't do any of these things comfortably as skirts would hold her back.

Therefore, school skirts actively hindered your activities nearly as much as the bustle did in the 1870s. You may worry that the wind might blow your skirt up (which often happens in the UK), you may feel the cold more, you may feel self-conscious showing your legs, you may attract unwanted attention and it can stop you feeling free.

Let's compare the number of decisions that males and females make on any given morning, whether they are going to school, college, work or out with friends.

You may have a day in the office, or a day meeting friends, but the decision-making process will be similar each day. You or your partner may have more or less steps to go through, so feel free to add your own steps to your own lists.

I believe women are also under pressure to vary their choice of clothes more, as it is noticed if you have worn a particular dress or an outfit before. I have evidence of this as when I committed the society 'sin' of forgetting what I wore for a previous event, a magazine editor made the point that "she loved that dress on me last time I wore it". Ouch!

There is even more pressure with the advent of social media, where a previous outfit can be easily viewed on your Instagram or Facebook page.

I can clearly recall the criticism that Princess Diana endured for re-wearing the same dress in the media in the 1980s. These days it is perceived as kinder to the planet to re-wear quality items. Perhaps Princess Diana was ahead of her time, or liked a particular dress, felt comfortable in it, found it practical to wear or was simply too fatigued to decide on another. Maybe she didn't remember she had worn it before, or she had more important matters to attend to.

The Impact

Having less decisions each day means that men have more headspace to think about wider issues. They can plan their time (or have it planned for them). Out of work time, they can have a lot more fun, be creative, be spontaneous, develop skills, do hobbies and attend courses. They can also focus on their personal development, watch the news or their favourite programme and learn practical skills if they choose. They can gain knowledge that can build up over time in the outside world and can add real value to their lives and their bank accounts.

However, no matter how efficient she is, I estimate a female may be in the bathroom getting ready for around 60 minutes and a male around 30 minutes. This often means they have less time to read about their favourite topic, watch their favourite programme, think creatively, learn about the latest in technology, pursue a hobby, find out what's on in the cinema or what's going on in the world outside their bedroom.

In short, men have more time to focus on the exterior world and gain knowledge and skills in that world. They also gain the confidence that comes with gaining and applying more knowledge and skills, whilst a woman is stuck repeating her efforts to look good.

By these calculations, women are spending around one hour per day extra, getting ready (to feel confident), be prepared and be well maintained, for the next social event, be it work, the school run or meeting with friends.

That's 60 minutes extra every single day. That's 60 minutes x 365 days per year = 21,900 minutes per year going around in circles. This is a minimum estimate, as you will probably spend more time before a night out, or twice a day when you get dressed in the morning, then get dressed again for a night out. Times that from when you are 13 to 73 so 60 years of getting ready.

That's 1,314,000 yes 1 Million +++ less time not reading about your favourite topic, not doing your favourite hobby, not learning more, not reading more, not writing more and not relaxing or developing yourself.

This is on average without looking after any children and not including the evening ritual of cleansing, toning and moisturising.

This is yet more weight of womanhood that we carry.

This is without clothes shopping online or trying on shoes in person, choosing a dress that suits you, trying different lipsticks to see if it goes with your colouring or coming out of the hairdressers with a terrible haircut. The choices are more than ever and so is the number of things that can go wrong.

Compare this with a man. They usually have two colours of shoes, brown or black low heeled, a few shirts, a couple of belts or a blue or black suit on average.

You may wonder why Simon Cowell from the X-Factor wears black T-shirts, black pants and black shoes in the morning.

He says his head is simply too full each day making business decisions and therefore choosing clothes would mean there are too many decisions for him to achieve what he would like to do in any one day. For him it's become his personal branding. Same hairstyle and same clothes. Job done. His mind is free for other, more strategic decisions and judging by his success, it has worked.

Now you may like to express your identity by being creative, being different, to stand out or conform, but at the end of the day this is a pressure imposed by society on mostly females. You might like to get ready while listening to your favourite songs, or think about scenarios in your day, or what questions you'd like to know the answers to, but chances are you will focus on what you need to wear, under time pressure, to get out the door for work or a meeting.

Too much time, money and effort is spent on womens' appearance. Why not spend 50% of that time going forwards, increasing our skills, knowledge or confidence in other ways, instead of going round in circles?

See the table below for the average male versus female decisions every day.

Male versus female decisions/steps/selections each day

Male decisions each day	Versus female decisions each day
Shower	Shower
Shave face	Shave body
Wash hair	Wash hair
Condition hair	Condition hair
Comb hair	Comb/brush hair
Dry hair	Dry hair
Style hair gel/mouse	Style hair gel/mouse
Style hair with hair spray	Style hair with hair spray
Brush teeth	Brush teeth
Floss teeth	Floss teeth
Moisturise face	Decide T-shirt/
Apply deodorant	jumper/blouse/vest top
Apply aftershave	Decide jacket
Decide which shirt/T-shirt/jumper	Decide trousers/jeans/canvas pants
Decide which jacket	Decide skirt

Male decisions each day	Versus female decisions each day
Decide Trousers/Jeans/ canvas pants	Decide dress
Decide underpants	Decide colour/ height /style of
Decide socks	shoes/boots/trainers
Decide shoes/trainers	Decide jacket/cardigan
Decide jacket/cardigan	Decide overcoat
Decide overcoat	Decide umbrella or not
Umbrella or not	Apply deodorant
	Cleanse face
	Tone face
	Moisturise face
	Prime skin
	Apply foundation
	Apply concealer
	Apply contour
	Apply highlighter
	Decide colour and apply blusher
	Apply face powder
	Apply eyebrow pencil
	Apply mascara layers, 1 or 2
	Apply eyeliner
	Decide & apply eyeshadow
	Decide & apply lipliner
	Decide & apply lipstick & top coat
	Decide earrings/ bracelet/necklace
	Apply perfume
	Remember makeup bag
	Remember any sanitary wear
	Remember medications
	Decide handbag

As you can see from the table above, in general, men have almost HALF the decisions per day that women do, even before they leave the bathroom. Could you add any more to the list? If so, how many? How much time does this take up in your life?

This daily decision making comes with the addition of weekly, two weekly, monthly, six weekly decisions etc. etc. to presenting yourself at social events. The list below is infinite to be honest, so feel free to add your own particular schedule to the following lists:

Weekly maintenance
Trim/file fingernails
Trim/file toenails
Pluck eyebrows
Whiten teeth
Exfoliate face
Face pack
Hair mask
False Tan
Drop off to/collect items from dry cleaners

Two/three weekly maintenance
Acrylic nails infills and repainted

Monthly maintenance
Waxing

Six weekly maintenance
Hair cut/coloured/styled
Teeth whitened

Three monthly maintenance
Botox
Filler

It is likely that you are in a habit that can be broken, given time and a bit of effort. It gets easier to form a new habit and gain a new skill, or more knowledge.

Take some time saving short cuts wherever possible, so wear a dress instead of a skirt and top, or get semi-permanent brows.

What you wear, or don't wear, has gained a lot of criticism and victim blaming over the years in the media and in the court room. In the next chapter let's look at how women are treated.

Ideas to Action

(1) Do you spend a lot of time doing your hair?

_____
_____

(2) Do you spend a lot of time planning your outfits?

_____
_____

(3) Do you spend a lot of time doing your makeup?

_____
_____

(4) Do you sometimes feel like you are going around in circles?

_____
_____

(5) Would you like to do other things?

_____
_____

(6) Do you spend a lot of time making appointments for feminine only issues?

_____
_____

(7) Does your partner spend a lot of time on self-presentation?

_____
_____

(8) Does your partner spend a lot of money on self-presentation?

_____
_____

(9) Would you like to learn or improve yourself more?

_____
_____

(10) Would you like to relax, do yoga or meditate more?

_____
_____

Actions to Empower

1. How much do you spend each month on personal care products?

2. How many minutes do you spend per day preparing your outfit?

3. How many minutes do you spend per day doing your hair?

4. How many minutes do you spend per day doing your makeup?

5. Calculate how much time per day you spend on how you look.

6. What hobby could you pursue with this extra time. such as an online/real life dance/exercise/yoga class or run/read/cycle?

7. Do an online course/read about the latest innovations/ learn to save and invest money for your future.

8. Prioritise connecting with a friend and arrange to meet up.

9. Give yourself positive self-talk, such as "I did well to arrange a meet up today."

10. Pat yourself on the arm while you say it out loud, for positive reinforcement.

CHAPTER 14

Harassment and Crimes Against Women

UNFORTUNATELY, AS GIRLS GROW up, it's sometimes a shock to see how they are treated outside of school.

You need only walk down the street as a young woman to be harassed.

In the 1970s and 80s, a group of builders hanging off scaffolding like apes, leering and shouting comments like 'phwoar' was considered a compliment, not the intimidating, unnerving and downright scary event it sometimes is.

From their perspective, it is often a bit of fun and banter with the lads.

If it's OK for a gang of men to behave like that, in daylight, without at least one intervening, then it's easy to see how this can easily occur on the street, in pubs and clubs today.

Would these same men be happy if their sister, girlfriend, wife, aunty, mother, cousin or friend was being cat called? Would they be comfortable with that?

Thankfully, it isn't seen as often now, as we have become more enlightened and it is seen as less acceptable.

However, it remains an unnerving experience on the pavement for young women. If my 16-year-old daughter walks down the street coming home from school in her school uniform, she often comes back with a tale of an old man being lecherous as she walks by.

Yesterday she walked down the street on a sunny day and a man of about 40/50, bald, fat and wearing sunglasses blatantly licked his top and bottom lips all the way along, as he looked her right in the eye. Enraged, I asked her what did she do? She said she moved round him, lowered her eyes and walked on as fast as she could.

My instinct as a mother was to kick him so hard where it would hurt or call him a paedophile loudly, but was talked down by my 16-year-old daughter.

It was clear she was already adept at recognising and avoiding these situations and getting away safely.

The same week my friend's daughter (17 years) was propositioned in a pub by a man aged about 40 who asked for her phone number. She said, "no thanks" and when she went to the toilet, he followed her down the corridor. Fortunately, a member of staff was in a room nearby, saw she was being harassed and followed her into the toilet where she had locked herself in the cubicle until this predatory male went away. The staff member stayed until he left. No complaint was made about the man.

I wonder now, why wasn't the police called? He should have been questioned, any video evidence obtained, photographed, or possibly named and shamed in public? This would then be on record and a picture could be built up of him, should anything similar or worse happen in the future, to show he has form for this creepy behaviour.

I wonder if it is such a common occurrence that this is accepted behaviour in bars?

If I was there at the time to speak to him myself, I would ask him what he thought he was doing. Did he have a sister, girlfriend, wife and how would be feel if an older man followed them into a dark corridor to do goodness knows what?

She had already said, "no thanks" so why didn't he get the message and leave her alone?

When I was around 13 or 14 years old, I remember a few events, in public places, in broad daylight, where older men would behave creepily and totally inappropriately.

Once I walked the dog and got some shopping for my mum on a sunny day and as I returned home with a badge on that was a freebie from a bread company which said, 'squeeze me I'm fresh' in big pink letters, an old man of about 60 shadowed me down the road. When I stopped to let him pass, he looked me in the eye, then looked at my badge and then back to me as if to say, 'come on'. Urgh. I didn't know exactly what this meant at the time, but I walked down that road as fast as I could, dragging my little dog with me.

Another time I walked with my cousin down the road, again on a sunny Sunday. When the roads were a bit quieter and another old man of around 50 literally opened his cliché raincoat and flashed. I didn't concentrate on his penis, but my eye was drawn to the look in his eyes as he sought my reaction. Full respect to my older cousin who was more streetwise than me and shouted at him loudly, "Is that all you've got?" to which he ran off.

I heard a quote from Margaret Atwood in the 1980s which said, "Men are afraid that women will laugh at them. Women are afraid that men will kill them." Should we publicly point and laugh at these men, so that other men know the repercussions of their actions are to be ridiculed, pointed at and laughed at? Would they quietly brood on this 'injustice' or insult to their ego and would women feel safe after this event, where they have simply called out the man's bad behaviour?

We didn't think to report it as we were probably in shock and were too embarrassed to tell our mums. I wonder now, how many girls he flashed to in his time? If we had reported it, would that have stopped him? Would he be on police records?

In my teenage years, it became more and more frequent for a time and I became less shocked and came to accept it as part of a young girl's life.

That same summer I came across another flasher. When my 14-year-old friend and I were walking up the street and looked up at the back row of a bus to see (again) a 40 or 50 year old man dangling his penis in front of us. We pointed and laughed at him as his eyes bore deep into our innocent souls.

I ask myself now, why didn't we run after the bus, write down or remember the number plate, bus number and time that the bus went past? Was it simply another of those days in our minds or was it that we were in shock and couldn't think clearly?

Those men thought they could get away with this creepy and intimidating behaviour. Unfortunately, they were right.

Have we created a culture where this behaviour is accepted? What if we couldn't run away? The very thought is disturbing to this day.

Why should WE be embarrassed by the inappropriate actions of some men in the community? We didn't know at the time, but it has been proved that behaviour like this often leads to other types of sexual harassment.

I spoke to Jane Kenyon, Founder of The Girls Out Loud charity, which seeks to empower young girls to use their voices and she suggested that as we always have our phones on us these days, we could take a photo for evidence in these circumstances (as long as it doesn't put us in any physical danger) and report it to the police.

Please tell your female friends to do this, as evidence is important. However, do not do this if you think it might escalate the situation and put you in further harm, your safety is more important.

Girls and women are often unprepared and in unexpected situations when these events happen. It is part of the control and the power imbalance that these males have planned or acted on - young girls innocently walking down the road in the sunshine or going to meet a friend.

There was no process in place and no number to call. Who knows how many times that man exposed himself and what he did next, but I am sure those victims have not exposed themselves to a 50 year old man.

I am not alone in my experiences but worse than this, the Metropolitan Police estimates that 1 in 5 women will experience sexual assault during their lifetime.

The cases of harassment are still common in the 2020s. If enough women report these instances, they will be counted and seen as the big problem it is and eventually resources will be allocated into reducing it.

Part of the problem is having proof as so many times, the woman is isolated, so then it becomes her word against theirs. However, it is estimated that only 3% are false reports according to Scotland Rape Crisis.org.uk 2021.

In 2020-21 The Metropolitan Police recorded more than 19,000 allegations of sexual offences[8]

The Police continue to promise to protect against such crimes, but it is a tall order and they can't do it on their own.

They say, "This must start with tackling society's tolerance of these awful crimes and associated behaviours."

Some police forces like Suffolk's 'Stay Safe' campaign seek to help report and reduce sexual assaults.

---

[8] *Metropolitan Police Website 'Violence against women and girls'.*

Other initiatives such as 'No More Excuses' by saferstreetscheshire.co.uk urges men to 'Stand with women not against them' with a remit to respect, understand and view women as equals.

They send buses around busy towns which contain equipment such as phone chargers, water and safety equipment for any incidents on the streets.

Reporting Crime

If crimes are to be reported by women, more resources and training are needed to deal with victims and to make it easier to report. Once the case goes to court, the victims should be treated in a way that doesn't put them through further trauma and does not question their past behaviour as a reason to discredit their claims. This would increase the number of convictions and penalties so that more women would be encouraged to come forward.

As a mother, I am saddened and enraged as this is not how it should be and this cannot go on unchecked for the next generation. Speaking to friends, it is not just women who are often in these situations it is teenagers and children.

I, for one, would vote for a government who put resources into changing our culture to educate males that this is unacceptable and they will face public shame and consequences if they behave like that.

I believe, this is what we need to do in society:

1. Increase the number of convictions for harassment.
2. Increase the number of convictions for flashing.
3. Increase the number of convictions for rape.
4. Believe the victim(s) and stop blaming them.
5. Increase legal resources.
6. Increase police resources.
7. Set up an accountable task force to get these criminals off the streets.
8 Communicate to the public that this is not acceptable either now or in the past.
9. Make reporting a crime easier.
10. Advertise a clear process for reporting crimes against women with timelines for acceptable responses, so that actions are taken promptly.

Women need to know the process and feel safe and supported when they do report a sexual crime. What do YOU think we need to do to protect women in society?

Part of the problem is that females are often disbelieved and consequently, their faith in the police and justice system is at an all-time low.

Criminals in the Media

I've just finished reading an article, 24 of the Most Notorious Criminals Jailed in the UK, Manchester Evening News (2 May 2022) by Fionnula Hainey[9].

---

[9] https://www.manchestereveningnews.co.uk/news/uk-news/24-most-notorious-criminals-jailed-20487964

A woman of 19 was named in the same article as a host of male criminals who had raped, drugged, murdered, threatened and subjected women to horrific abuse before being captured and imprisoned.

Her 'crime' was to have been distracted by a phone call when she left her baby son in the bath. She was jailed for 22 months because he slipped out of his bath seat and drowned. Tragic for the baby, tragic for the mother who will probably be grieving for the rest of her life. She was charged with gross negligence and manslaughter. She called emergency services and tried to resuscitate him. She said it was her 'fault' to the emergency services as she had allowed herself to be distracted. She was given an immediate custodial sentence.

How could this accident be put on the same list as rapists, murderers, wife abusers, child abusers and stalkers whose crimes were often premeditated and vicious? One jealous husband had stabbed his wife 300 times and another had murdered and dismembered a woman after a night out.

Treatment of Women in Court

For instances of historic abuse, this is particularly difficult to pin down and make a robust case without evidence. Some lawyers even recommend that the cases are not reported because the trauma that the victim may go through when reporting it and possibly appearing in court, would be equal or worse than the crime itself, as their actions, what they wore, their sexual history and their reputation is often questioned more minutely than the rapist's. Victim blaming at its worst.

Added to this, the victim has tried to forget the abuse but will remember a face, smell, touch, feelings, intonation or looks and the experience will mark their future relationships forever.

Remember the public trial of Amber Heard and Johnny Depp? She was under such scrutiny that she is now in Spain to process the after effects of the trial which has had a huge impact on her life and career. It feels like a cautionary tale to other potential abuse victims, so therefore women will be even more reluctant to go on trial to prosecute any man.

The legal and financial abuse of Britney Spears has been an ongoing story in the media. How could one of the richest, most powerful and high-profile women in the world be enslaved for over 13 years? It shows that if she can be abused (by her own father), then anyone can. If no-one did anything about it for over a decade, what hope is there for the rest of us?

It has been shown that in the eyes of the law, the onus is on the victim to prove an injustice. Added to this, the victim is often isolated, weakened, threatened, sometimes even drugged and bribed, so you can clearly see how the system is stacked against them.

A man's right to have sex with his wife was part of the marriage contract in the past. They were handed over by their fathers to 'be looked after', however, in reality it was also to have sex as a conjugal right, bear children, cook, tidy, clean and make a comfortable home for the man of the house.

A 'successful' marriage contract was one where the daughter was married off to a rich man, whether he was ancient, kind or abusive.

In most cultures, once the girl was married, she could not go back to her family, no matter what she had married into, as this was seen as shameful for her family. She was seen as the failure, so she was told to 'make the best of the situation' so again she was isolated, unable to talk about it, unable to get support and unable to escape.

It seems the old tradition of women being owned by their fathers and then given away to their husbands (like cattle) has continued in the 2020s and women are still seen as property in many cultures.

If we are not treated as individual humans, then how can we forge our own identities and realise our potential?

In the next chapter, let's look at healthy and equal relationships.

Ideas to Action

(1) How can we teach boys and young men to respect and support females?

(2) Can you get a group of girls, women, boys and men together to discuss everyday harassment?

(3) What are the repercussions?

(4) How do we go about changing everyday harassment?

(5) How can we put pressure on the government, businesses and individuals to call out this behaviour until it is no longer acceptable?

(6) How can you draw attention and stop these behaviours in businesses?

(7) Ask your local police force how they encourage women to report assaults?

(8) Do you feel safe walking the streets alone at night?

(9) Do you feel okay about your daughter walking the streets at night?

(10) Ask your local police force how they deal with domestic crimes against women.

Actions to Empower

1. Have you had any experiences of sexual harassment in the past?

2. How did you deal with it and what would you do if it happened again?

3. Have you been abused or raped or know anyone who has?

4. What did you/they do in response - fight, flight or freeze?

5. What would you do to protect yourself now?

6. Ask your children, have they experienced harassment.

7. Have you any evidence?

8. If so, report it to the police.

9. Give yourself positive self-talk, such as "I did well to confront this issue today."

10. Give yourself and / or your child, a hug. It is NEVER our fault.

CHAPTER 15

Relationships

IF YOU LOVE YOURSELF and your life, then you're in a good place to meet a partner. Once you've found them and have fallen in love and are happy with how they treat you, then you may decide to move in, as a natural step in the relationship.

Partnerships

You will need to be clear about what you need from them so the partnership starts off with mutual respect and mutual benefit so both gain equal value from being in the relationship. You need to realise your own worth and be happy without too much compromise on either side.

The expectations and habits you set early on in a relationship will be the ones that endure. Once you start with any habit, particularly ones detrimental to yourself, your needs, hopes and dreams, then these bad habits will continue over time.

Even today, I still see a younger, better-looking woman marrying an older, wealthier man.

This model of partnership has been copied for decades when it was socially acceptable and even encouraged by family and friends - an inexperienced and beautiful younger woman would marry an older, richer and more powerful man as a trade-off.

I hope that as the years go on and my daughters get older, this scenario is seen less and less as society develops, women harness their own personal power, get good jobs and earn their own money. As a result, their partnerships will become more equal.

I also hope the cliché of a successful man swapping his wife for a younger model as a symbol of his power, wealth or status, will be seen as a sign of insecurity, to be pitied by male friends, instead of the scenario of getting an envious look or a 'pat on the back' from misogynistic peers.

Girls are often told they should be 'nice' but it holds us back in the interior and exterior world. Next time you are thinking of being 'nice' think about being assertive instead.

Being nice enables others to get what they want. It doesn't get you what you want in life.

Division of Labour

When you are planning who will do what in the home, try not to fall into the trap of doing 'pink' or 'blue' jobs.

The skilled 'blue' jobs might be drilling a hole in the wall to put up a picture or building a new piece of furniture by putting pieces of wood, screws and plastic together. These jobs are irregular but have more satisfaction as they solve a problem, which is high on Maslow's triangle.

In my experience, if a man was to tackle a DIY job, then he would take pleasure in also buying the tools to do it.

Whereas a woman would often try to do a DIY job without investing in the right tools and when she failed would blame herself. For example, I once tried to take down a full set of fitted wardrobes when I was heavily pregnant with a manual screwdriver, so what should have taken one hour, took six hours, I kid you not!

I've recently bought a charging drill in a carry box with all the different heads for different sized screws and honestly it is empowering to carry a drill in your hand as it whizzes round to complete a job. It is such a time saver and a definite BUZZ! Get one for yourself and use it with pride and precision. It can easily be a 'pink' job!

However, the traditional 'pink jobs' are typically repetitive, low-skilled chores, that cover the hygiene factors (you notice if they are NOT done, but not if they ARE done, so they are largely invisible). They are a lot lower on Maslow's triangle in terms of satisfaction.

There's even a cleaning product called 'the pink stuff' branded in bright pink containers which is eye-catching and pitched unapologetically to the female. Where's the blue version?

In a balanced relationship, it would be beneficial to both parties to reassess these colour coded roles.

What about taking on tasks that you enjoy and are good at? The chances are your likes will be complementary to your partner.

Does your partner like cooking? Give them the responsibility for cooking for the family. Do you prefer doing the laundry? You do that task and so it goes on...!

This will also enable each partner to do tasks they don't mind so much, or if they choose the cooking option, it can allow them downtime from a stressful, mentally taxing job. They can focus on something simple and be in the present, which has been proven to de-stress and use a different part of the brain which is also beneficial to mental health.

A partnership includes communication and negotiation. Obviously, it will change over time but for the most part, if one person has the responsibility (not just the task of doing the washing) this takes away the mental burden of identifying what job needs to be done and when, for example, instead of a nudge to your partner to remember to do the washing, as well as the physical task itself, they are responsible for that area, so your brain is free to focus on something else.

You need to be clear about what is expected from both partners.

If you take on more household chores, you will lose more of your time and identity.

Relationship Needs

We all need different qualities from our partners as well as trust and honesty.

If you went into a business partnership, you would write a list of pros and cons, strengths and weaknesses and what you would both gain by being in a partnership together.

Years ago, pre-nuptials were seen as a cynical start to a marriage, but to start from a position of clarity and honesty surely is a good start to any relationship. What do you think?

It would also make sense to do a similar analysis for your personal partnership, to be clear on what you need and gain from the partnership and vice versa.

Sometimes these needs are not identified until they rear their ugly heads when they are not satisfied, but honestly how are YOUR needs going to be satisfied if you can't say what they are?

Keep it private if you wish, but make sure you are honest about it as the only person you would be fooling is yourself.

There are only 24 hours in each day, but many women with a full-time role do their paid job, get up early and do their unpaid jobs of tidying or cleaning the house, washing clothes, ironing school uniforms (pleated skirts argh), making sandwiches or preparing the evening meal in a slow cooker – this is the physical side. Then there's the mental energy to think about what to have for dinner, who likes what, writing a shopping list etc. This is known as a 'second shift'.

Added to this, there's the emotional energy to put into whatever happens minute by minute, it could be supporting a sobbing child or phoning a lonely family member. The list is endless and often falls to the woman.

So from when a woman moves in with a man, her daily timetable changes to a life revolving around and caring for others.

Marriage

TV and film have shown a lot of gender stereotyping over the years, but are they merely a barometer of the time they are written?

Young children love Disney films, where they are guaranteed to have a happy ending, but are they deeper than that? Do they overtly and covertly show us the path to being a serving Princess, as every girl 'should' want to be a princess, right?

The Princess concept is deeply flawed, for example in Beauty and the Beast, she is expected to be beautiful, but he is a beast. He is ugly, but as an entrapped female, she falls in love with him, despite his physical features, tantrums and selfish behaviour. The key to escape from his own torture is for someone to love him. She also puts him and his needs first and only escapes to put the needs of her father, who has ill health, ahead of her own. She has no escape.

Is there any male in film that acts like this? I can't think of one, but please let me know on Instagram if there is.

Another clear message I got was that Princesses have struggles and a need to escape (from the slavery and injustice of their earlier lives) before they meet their Prince.

If you take this message further, and want to meet your own Prince, then the memo is clear, act like a Princess to attract your Prince. However, in real life that is reversed as that's often when a life of domestic slavery begins.

You were free and independent before marriage. You were free to have a messy room, wear clothes that didn't need ironing, free to hoover up once a week, or just when you had visitors. Free to shop when you liked, eat when you liked and slob around in your pyjamas. Free of makeup, magic pants and push up bras. Free from long lashes and high heels. Free to be your natural self.

Traditionally, there is an expectation to change your surname and take on the name of your male partner and this is celebrated in society as the new Mrs B etc. However, this also means that you have the added admin of changing your name on bills, passports and insurances etc.

Once we change our name we also lose a part of our identity. No wonder we struggle!

All of a sudden you are expected to take on the job of managing the diary and with that comes managing not just your own diary, but your partner's diary. In that diary is a lot of other dates and birthdays you didn't know before, such as their family's birthdays. Then it's organising people and dates to meet up, appropriate cards to choose, to buy, to write, to get others to sign, to buy a stamp for and to post. Hence the popularity of moonpig.com to send a last minute or personalised card or present.

Having spoken to many friends, this seems to be an unspoken rule in the marriage contract, even now.

Then there's the added burden of organising a meet-up with friends and family, whether it's for drinks or a four-course dinner. Mostly it's the woman who flags up it's time to see family or friends again. Then it's the:

- What shall we cook?
- How many courses?
- Are they vegetarian?
- Are they pescatarian?
- Are they vegan?
- What is their favourite food?
- Any allergies or dislikes to consider?
- What's their least favourite food?
- Do they drink alcohol?
- Do they like red wine/white wine/prosecco?
- Who does the shopping, who does the personalised, thoughtful, appreciated or unappreciated extras, like setting the table?

And the list goes on....

Who does the cleaning, the tidying, the hoovering, the polishing and the washing up? Who gets the posh glasses out, the crockery, the cutlery, sets the table, then clears up, washes up, scrubs the pots and the pans or wipes up any stains or mess along the way?

Start as you mean to go on especially when agreeing to do the following chores:

Meal planning - This is exhausting and repetitive so take it in turns to plan the week's food, which would make it more interesting and give responsibility to each partner.

Cooking - You might start off loving it as it's a novelty (I NEVER did) but it can very quickly get tiring and boring. There are some good recipe delivery companies out there like Hello Fresh, so do yourself a favour and treat yourself if you can or take it in turns.

Cleaning the Home - there's the everyday cleaning, washing the dishes or loading the dishwasher, unloading the dishwasher, wiping counter tops to eradicate crumbs and stickiness, which has to be done five times a day in my experience.

Train the other members of your household early on to clean up after themselves or face your wrath, they will soon do it as habit and their future partners will be better off for it too.

Decorating - painting of walls and furniture can be done quite easily with the latest sprays and paints from matt to full on glitter walls, but more skilled jobs like wallpapering are probably best left to the experts. Brownie points to you if you can do it, add to the list of skills you bring!

DIY - doing a proper job that you would pay someone to do.

Gardening - make the time to do it yourself or if you can, find a good gardener and pay them.

House Maintenance - finding tradespeople, getting quotes, negotiating a price, choosing someone, booking a convenient date, supervising them, making drinks, inspecting the work, calling them or re-booking them for any snags and paying them.

Food Shopping - choosing meals for a week taking everyone's needs and wants into consideration. Making a list, deciding a budget, remembering shopping bags, travelling to the supermarket, parking, finding a coin to borrow a trolley and buying what is on the list in budget. Going around the shop, looking for good deals, looking for items on the list, putting them in the basket, putting them on the conveyor belt and paying for them. Putting them in the shopping bags, putting it into the car, putting the trolley back and then taking it out of the car. Putting it in the correct cupboards, fridge or freezer, unless you take a few shortcuts and order online.

Washing clothes – Organising the washing so it is ready for school. Sorting the dirty laundry into colours and setting and loading the washing machine. Unloading the washing machine, putting it on the line or the dryer. Taking it out of the dryer or washing line, sorting and folding it and putting it away in the right drawers.

Ironing or steaming clothes - making them crease free to look presentable and not burning them.

Are tasks equally shared in your household?

For example, speaking at the nail bar recently, one of the joint owners (married couple) admitted she does EVERYTHING around the house. She does all the daily planning, tidying, cooking, cleaning, washing, ironing, planning holidays, planning social life, admin for child one, admin for child two, school uniforms, school run, dropping off at clubs, picking up from clubs and standing in a field for two hours come rain or shine to watch child(ren) do their weekly sports match.

She admitted that she was EXHAUSTED! And no wonder!

I asked, "Why do you do all that?" She said, "It's easier than shouting and asking for the umpteenth time." Now this is either a very clever trick of the children and husband to go deaf and blind, or they expect that these jobs are for mothers only.

She is a strong, successful and determined businesswoman, but I suspect she has set up a poor deal in the household and even worse, she is enabling it by continuing to do so. Do you do this?

Another woman complained that she did everything around their home and I asked her why and she said that "things would not be done to my standards". Maybe she could have a more balanced life if she relaxed her standards a little. Is this you?

What would happen if we turned this situation around? Or shared some of the responsibilities? Does this happen in your household?

How would you view a man who cooked, cleaned, shopped, looked after the children, thought about their favourite meals, did the school run, remembered to buy or make clothes for international book day, helped make bonnets for easter etc. Would you respect them or cherish them? Take them for granted? Or laugh at them for being 'a mug'?

This everyday chat really resonated with me and being menopausal also made me a little bit angry. I too had enabled my family to behave like this and be a modern-day Cinderella and even worse, I had set it up like this. I could not remember one single person telling me a mother does this or that, but I had slowly and insidiously absorbed it from social situations and fairy stories as a baby, to seeing my own mum do two jobs taking care of and managing the whole household from administration, budgeting, decision making, shopping, social planning, car maintenance, managing insurances, polishing shoes, cooking, cleaning, washing, ironing (and that was just in one day).

After this conversation I decided to put it to the test myself and simply ask my family members to do something.

I went to the supermarket (I've perfected this to one hour for one week's shopping).

It was a Monday morning in the school holidays, so I thought great, may as well start the week as I mean to go on!

I got home chuckling to myself at my cunning plan, ha! It got to about 4pm and I asked my youngest 13 year old would she cook dinner that night and she said, "Yes." It was that simple. "What is for dinner?", she asked. "I don't know," I said. "Look in the fridge". She said, "Is beef teriyaki, okay?". This was a quick stir fry meal I'd bought and guess what, it was the best dinner I have ever had. Could you do this?

People simply can't read your mind, so you must learn to communicate your thoughts and feelings and USE YOUR VOICE to ask.

The benefit of this scenario is that I got the joy of having an evening off cooking and she got the satisfaction of being able to cook for herself and others. She had started her journey to independence and developed skills and confidence for life. It really is a win-win situation.

Please try it yourself and if they don't do it first time, then ask a second time. Perhaps show them the first time so they feel supported. Now obviously you can't ask a young child to cook on their own without fear of a terrible accident, but depending on their age and ability they can probably put bread in the toaster and heat up some beans in the microwave. That's another meal sorted right there.

You don't HAVE to be a slave in your own home so please don't.

Multi-tasking has been shown to be an inefficient use of your brain and energies, as your brain has to zoom down in to one task, then zoom out again, ten zoom in again to do another task, then zoom out again to do another task. It is exhausting too and not the best use of your time, effort or energy.

By doing most of the mundane and menial tasks you are seen as lower status in society and if you don't value yourself, then society won't value you either and when society doesn't value you then you don't value yourself and so this status quo continues.

Here is a list to start the conversation and ensure happiness in the home where partner A and partner B have tasks to do in their shared home.

This also ensures that both have time to recharge and relax with a treat or self-care, be it an hour in the bath or an hour on the drums.

Now that you have reallocated your time, let's look at your options for your career and how to earn more cash to give you a better quality of life.

Ideas to Action

Think about the practical help you bring to the partnership, such as diary management

1. ———————————————
2. ———————————————
3. ———————————————
4. ———————————————
5. ———————————————
6. ———————————————
7. ———————————————
8. ———————————————
9. ———————————————
10. ———————————————

What practical help do you need from your partner?

1. ———————————————
2. ———————————————
3. ———————————————
4. ———————————————
5. ———————————————
6. ———————————————
7. ———————————————
8. ———————————————
9. ———————————————
10. ———————————————

Actions to Empower

Put your colour coded initials against each task to help share the following tasks equally:-

Daily

(1) Make bed (if you have children 8 upwards, they can straighten their own duvet and plump their pillows) ☐

(2) Sort mail and action it. ☐

(3) Pick-up clutter, put away and wipe work tops in kitchen. ☐

(4) Load dishwasher. ☐

(5) Empty dishwasher. ☐

(6) Pick up clutter and put items away from shared rooms. ☐

(7) Clear and clean dining table and placemats ready for the next meal. ☐

(8) ☐

(9) ☐

(10) ☐

(11) ☐

(12) ☐

Twice a week

(1) Sanitise toilet. ☐

(2) Empty kitchen and recycling bins. ☐

(3) ☐

(4) ☐

(5) ☐

(6) ☐

Fortnightly

(1) Polish mirrors/TV/windows/tables. ☐

(2) ☐

(3) ☐

Actions to Empower

Weekly

(1) Dust surfaces, in the bedrooms, living room, dining room and hall. ☐

(2) Clean shower/bath/basin/toilet/hoover/mop bathroom. ☐

(3) Tidy/hoover/mop kitchen. ☐

(4) Plan meals for the week. ☐

(5) Grocery shop for the week. ☐

(6) Fill car with petrol/diesel/electricity. ☐

(7) Empty house bins, fill outside bins and put onto road for emptying & bring them in. ☐

(8) Wash clothes and bedding. ☐

(9) Change bedding. ☐

(10) Tidy/hoover/polish own bedroom. ☐

(11) Take clothes to laundry and sort into: Blues and green/pinks, reds and oranges/black and darks/whites and creams together. ☐

(12) Wash/dry clothes/fold clothes/put in baskets. ☐

(13) Put away own washing from baskets. ☐

(14) ☐

(15) ☐

(16) ☐

(17) ☐

(18) ☐

Monthly

(1) Clean car or take to be cleaned. ☐

(2) Clean oven. ☐

(3) Clean out fridge and put of out-of-date foods into bins or composter. ☐

(4) Clean microwave. ☐

(5) ☐

CHAPTER 16

Finding a Career
(Post Children)

IN A CAPITALIST SOCIETY, your 'value' in society is largely decided by how much you earn or your job status.

We don't have 'penis envy' as thought by Sigmund Freud, but we probably have power envy as we navigate this patriarchal world that seems to be stacked against the female and set up for the male to enjoy a good salary.

As a woman you have big decisions to make once you have children, which you are not always informed about *before* you become pregnant.

What you should know is that when you become pregnant, life as you know it is about to be knocked down and rebuilt as you start again as a new family.

Therefore you need a clear plan with good practical, emotional and mental support. You also need friends and family you can trust to help you on this unknown and challenging new adventure. I cannot stress this enough.

Will you continue your career in the company you are in, in a different company, stay full-time, go part-time, become a stay at home parent, retrain or make a complete career change?

Quite often as a woman, the decision is made for you. You may be made redundant, your role may no longer be viable, as you can't do long hours, travel far or work weekends due to family commitments. You may ask for part-time hours and get them, but let's face it, they may be part-time hours and part-time pay, but you will still have to be flexible and adapt to doing extra hours when the children are in bed, so you will find yourself writing emails or texting the team way into the evening.

Humans are born, procreate and die. How is this not factored into working life?

If you manage to secure a part-time role around school hours or term time, you will be paid a lot less than your qualifications or experience deserve. Many companies take advantage of this fact under the guise of being family friendly.

Beware! If you are off work on maternity leave, or take extended leave whilst your children are young, then it is much more difficult to step back into the world of work in a new career as you might need retraining first.

And too often you may have to take a backward step in your career to fit hours around your children's school, so will be earning less.

This is still the accepted norm in society, as most women in heterosexual relationships generally still earn less than the male partner.

Hopefully, countries leading the way such as Iceland, where women are striking to achieve equal pay and respect, will spread to other countries and lead to action in the wider world for equal pay, equity and respect.

If you had difficulty finding a career before children, then after children, it's likely to be a lot harder.

If you have left work or 'lost' your job, it may be a good idea to try a new approach in your job hunt.

If there's a company you like the sound of, or a job role that you have always wanted to do, why not ask a company if you could shadow someone there? By doing this, they can find out about you, you can find out about them and learn some new skills, without the pressure of having to perform straight away in a paid role. You will also build up some contacts and network with people in the industry.

You will also find out whether you would like the paid role and you will see what personal qualities are required in the company culture as well as practical skills. You will get to know if the company is expanding and any future development opportunities. Don't forget this method is like a long interview, so you will have to dress appropriately and perform to impress them to be offered a paid job or to earn a great reference.

There must be a calculation of how much it costs to recruit, train and shadow a new employee until they are fully competent, versus how much it costs to maintain their skilled ones. Has anyone done it? Could you do it?

The reality is that there is often a skills 'leak' post maternity leave.

I challenge the head of any company to be progressive, moral and practical with the opportunity to retain experienced and skilled employees by offering support, flexible working patterns, a phased introduction back to work and fair pay.

Does this happen in your company? Could you make these changes in your company?

Mature females offer both life and communication skills. They are well rounded, practical and experienced, which increases their value in any team. Collaborative working, communication and cheerleading of individuals in teams have been described as feminine or soft skills. These skills mean they also excel at listening when having conversations with customers. Experience and knowledge helps build important customer relationships.

Therefore, if you are in a position to help another female (who no doubt has had to endure a lot of suppression in life) then always give them support, a leg up or a kind word of encouragement. Or, be a mentor, or sponsor them by giving them a well paid job. You will find it so rewarding – it's such a win-win situation.

YOUR OPTIONS

Work Outside of the Home

a) Part-time work in same company before pregnant

If you choose to work part-time, be aware that these roles are like hen's teeth in the workplace. If you can ask your current employer to do this, who knows your work ethic, your strengths and your skills, this would probably be your best choice if you, like most women are continuing to work outside of the home as well.

I say this as the building blocks in your life have been knocked down, to have the familiarity of the same job, same employees and same route, no matter its faults, can be important in the transition from single human to new mum who needs a secure support system.

Unfortunately, the experience of many women is that they will probably be expected to do a part-time job in full-time hours.

You will likely feel guilty when you are at work (for leaving your baby) and guilty when you have your baby (for not keeping up at work) and not be able to attend most social events after work.

Therefore, you will probably feel out of the communication loop of what is going on in the workplace.

It is helpful to recognise these feelings of guilt that many women feel and try to rationalise and counteract them, which will reduce stress too.

The best advice I ever got was to try to be fully in the moment you are in. Therefore, if you are in a baby club, it is an absolute luxury to be out of paid work and nurturing a beautiful new human. For example, if you are attending a baby massage class, breathe in the smell of the oils, treasure the touch of your baby's super soft skin and enjoy these moments as best you can, if you have been up throughout the night or not, as sooner than you think you will be on to the next stage of life.

You will likely experience a knock to your status and your confidence, as you are not in the office all the time and forging the same relationships you did. You will probably be tired and feel differently towards work and colleagues, as your priorities change and your perceived value to the company may be less.

Therefore, you may start to doubt yourself and value yourself less, despite you doing a whole lot more.

Be kind to yourself and prioritise your own needs for rest and support too,

b) Part-time work in another role or company

This is also an option, but be aware that in this position you may have less responsibility and more flexibility than you did before in a full-time job, but:

- You will probably earn less per hour than you did before.
- You will probably have to do more hours than you are paid for.
- You will have more responsibility than you are paid for.
- You may be looked down on by other full-time employees as you are 'only part-time'.
- You might not have the same opportunities for career progression.
- You probably won't have the same opportunities to learn new skills or go on courses for enrichment.
- You probably won't have many new skills to put on your CV as your time is limited.
- You will be contributing less into your pension pot for the future.

You are brave to try a new part time role, despite juggling children, a home and hopefully a supportive partner.

But you may have to re-prioritise your life as the focus is now on the main wage earner as they will be keeping the roof over your family's head and paying the bills.
However, be aware that you are still partners and need to communicate how you think, act and feel.

If you do not have a partner, it may be easier to plan your week, as you will have fewer people to take into account, but you may struggle for mental support, emotional support and practical support and less cash to pay the bills for you and your child(ren).

c) Full-time work

You may like to continue in the job you love, or you may have no option if you are a single parent or away from the support of family and friends.

This can be challenging if you do not have support nearby and someone to pick up the baton of responsibility and practical support if you need to work late, or you are stuck in traffic or you are simply exhausted.

If it is a choice, then the pros should outweigh the cons, so write them down clearly and think about them.

What will happen if your child is sick? What about sports days? Drop off and pick up? There are 3 levels of planning - the physical, mental and emotional elements which need to be addressed to enable you to function in your exterior role, especially if it is high stress and busy.

You may decide that it is the right decision whilst the children are in nursery school which tends to close around 6pm, but this may change when your children start school and they need to be collected at 3.30pm.

If you are in a well paid job, fully investigate having a nanny or child care for wraparound care such as before and after school clubs, so that you are reassured that the practicalities are covered.

Emotionally you should seek support from friends and relatives as it could be tough at the start, or you may be happy to return to the normality of your life before children.

The mental load will also be challenging as you try to remember school events, organise outfits and find out about your children's new teachers, friends and their parents.

You need to plan regular rest or you will feel resentful or suffer burn out.

d) Working for Yourself

Despite working tremendously hard during the day and having little sleep during the night, a lot of women use this time 'off' work to start their own business which fits around family life, so that they can do the school pick up and drop off, then work in the evening when the kids have gone to bed.

Although it is exhausting at the time, long term it could offer you greater rewards as the profits are all yours should it be a success.

It is also more rewarding as you have more scope to be creative, spontaneous and can problem solve.

If you work at home or alone, you can counteract this by finding great networking groups online or going to shared office spaces, so that you can focus on your plans to make money for the family.

This might seem like another planet after being at home under a mountain of nappies, but it is a good option for women these days so be assured that there will be plenty of Mums in the same position, so you will receive a lot of support and tips to help you.

If they can do it, then so can you. It's good to know that if you see someone else achieving, then you realise you can achieve too. Whatever it is, it helps to be around people who are in similar situations, achieving their goals and heading where YOU want to be.

Paternity Leave

Despite the UK statutory paternity leave policy of up to two weeks paid paternity leave, many men do you take up this offer, due to the company culture and pressure to behave like a strong male, or they simply cannot afford to. In October 2023, men are entitled to the lower amount of either £172.48 or 90% of their average weekly earnings per week.

This masculine coding is also a system where men would rather die from suicide or a heart attack brought on by stress, than admit they have emotional needs or issues. They may feel they cannot take time off in case they are perceived as weak or not showing full commitment to their career, so may miss out on future career progression opportunities in a competitive job market.

If they don't share the load in terms of childcare and stay at home to bond with their children, then they begin a habit of leaving the family home to focus purely on financial responsibility instead of living a more balanced life.

There is no shame in showing that you have emotional needs although it takes courage. Men have it hard too.

Men need to be able to show they are human, to feel able to spend time with their children, connect emotionally, communicate and give practical and emotional support to their partner.

We are humans together.

In the next chapter, you can see how men tend to follow one path and women become more entrenched in societal norms so become #Motherhooded.

Ideas to Action

(1) Look at the options above and think about your finances.

(2) Consider full-time, part-time or one of you staying at home.

(3) Who could/would want to be the SAHP?

(4) Think about what is best for you.

(5) Think about what is best for your children.

(6) Think what is best for your partner (if you have one).

(7) How will you ensure you retain your own identity and independence?

(8) How will the SAHP get a rest as it is hard work, day in day out without breaks?

(9) You may wish to trial your options. Is it possible to trial your options?

(10) Is your partner involved and onboard with the new phase of life?

Actions to Empower

1. If you are going back to work after children, plan how you are going to keep your skills up to date so do this online or by speaking to HR.

2. Read the latest news around your industry.

3. Investigate a career change. What are the pros and cons?

4. Find out from friends, family or the news which companies are family friendly.

5. Ask your old colleagues if there are family friendly roles in their company.

6. Write a one year plan for you, your career and your family.

7. Write a 2-5 year plan for you, your career and your family.

8. Write a 5-10 year plan for you, your career and your family.

9. Give yourself a positive affirmation, such as "I am a skilled and experienced employee."

10. Pat yourself on the arm while you say it out loud, for positive reinforcement.

CHAPTER 17

Motherhooded
©2024

IF YOU CHOOSE TO be a mother and are lucky enough to become pregnant, the news is celebrated by everyone, but no-one tells you about the horrors of giving birth and the aftermath. It seems like the whole of humankind conspires to keep you from the grim reality for a lot of women.

It's like if they did tell you the terrible truth, the human race would die out. I believe it surely would.

Deep, regular and excruciating pain hails the start of the process, whereby the largest muscle in a woman's body contracts. It is these inner muscles, from the top of the uterus, which press down on the baby's bottom and in turn, the baby's head presses down on your cervix (which is the opening of the uterus). The cervix starts to dilate to get ready for the baby's head and body to be forced out of the vagina in childbirth.

Despite going into hospital and being waited on with cups of tea and drugs on hand, it is no holiday and the exhaustion of growing a baby inside you is replaced with the shock of contractions when the time is ready for your baby to arrive.

Luckily the hormone oxytocin is also pumped around your body which works to pacify your usually busy, questioning brain with questions like "How is this huge melon sized human going to come out of my body?" Well, the usual answer is with pain and stitches!

If the woman is lucky, the pain spent in childbirth will produce a healthy and beautiful baby.

Unfortunately, no male can incubate and give birth to a baby on this planet (except for a sea horse).

However, human male partners CAN take a role in physically looking after their baby and child post birth trauma. So why are the vast majority of women still responsible for the primary physical, emotional and wellbeing care duties of their children on a daily basis?

The weight of managing a child (or children) as well as household management, teaching of skills like walking, talking and running, developing social skills, counselling, coaching, driving, enabling, planning, scheduling and basically the project management of a new human from birth to adulthood (so a minimum of 18 years per child) falls on the woman a huge majority of the time. (See Mumsnet).

Thus, often after she has been #Womanhooded, she is then #Motherhooded.

Whilst the male still bears the financial stress of supporting the family the majority of the time.

Without doubt, children are a blessing and a miracle. They give cuddles, love and deep satisfaction, but not without a whole lot of care, thought and emotion.

When a partner returns from their work outside the home, they can take their turn inside the home, as although unpaid and undervalued, the woman who takes parental leave has been working all day, often without a break, to take care of the baby.

She has probably been up throughout the night to breastfeed, often cleaning, organising and tidying the house, shopping for supplies, planning and making dinner and taking 5 minutes to wash, dress and apply any makeup and comb or style her hair or even go to the toilet. This is a constant physical, mental and emotional drain on her energy levels.

Multi-tasking like this is a demanding juggling act, which often continues for many years until the child(ren) can be left alone in a room for 10 minutes without the all-encompassing fear that they are going to kill themselves by falling off a chair or banging their head on a hard floor.

Until society and individuals see that males and females should bear equal load and take shared responsibility for each child, each day, then young humans will not benefit from the two styles of parenting and these so called 'softer' skills will not be valued.

Males and females bring different qualities, styles of parenting and role models to each child's upbringing. By taking turns, the other person can take a break and come back refreshed and both parents can benefit from a deeper connection with their child, but this is far from a societal norm even in 2024.

When you care for your child(ren) you learn to appreciate the hard work that the other parent does and can be more empathetic and appreciative along the parenting journey, whilst developing bonds between the child and the parent. Does this happen in your home?

It has been proven that when hugging a child, the heartbeat of the child can reduce stress in the adult. A fast (or stressed) heartbeat in the adult will be slowed down when hugging the child, to be in sync with the slower heartbeat. This is just one example of the healing nature of a hug from a child. There are infinite physical, emotional and mental benefits for both the child and the adult as they bond together.

Stay at Home Mum

If you have the option, it might make financial sense to stay at home. When you calculate childcare costs (which alone may be as much as your mortgage) plus other costs such as buying clothes, lunches, shoes, travel and car parking costs, you may decide to stay at home with your children if it is at all an option.

However, you should be aware that it will be a totally different life from your previously independent one. You may or may not like it, so you need to think carefully about what would be best for YOU and your whole family.

As we live in a capitalist society, where your value as an individual is based on what you earn, what car you drive or what brand of bag you carry, you should be aware that your status in society will drop considerably.

You will further lose your identity as you will be called your child's mum in your new world of new friends and teachers. You may have a PhD but you will be addressed as 'Jenny's Mum'.

As well as this loss of individual identity, you will experience broken sleep. Your addled body and brain will then have to multi-task all the new jobs that lie in front of you in the day ahead, such as cleaning and tidying the home. Your new Mum life will revolve around feeding your baby and changing nappies.

You will likely forget the names of the other women you meet under these stresses. The low point for me was when I could not remember the name of the mum who I passed twice a day and chatted to a lot. After plucking up the courage to admit that I had forgotten her name (again) she told me it was Jo, the same as mine. I had literally forgotten my own name! ARGH! That's the effect that inadequate sleep has on your brain!

In addition, you will also have less money than you are used to, so you will have to budget well and learn how to find bargains or second-hand goods.

There will also be a shift of power in your relationship, as the wage earner and the non-wage earner.

Sharing Childcare

In your new tired state, you will also assume that after the kids, the wellbeing of your partner is more important than your own, as they are the one paying the rent or mortgage and literally keeping the roof over your heads.

Therefore, their shirts will be washed and conditioned before your crumpled T-shirts are even thought about and their dinners will be large and nutritious while you will likely get by on cold coffee and leftovers as little by little you become a 'good mum' or in other words, #Motherhooded.

This can be a trap you can both easily fall into, so learn to assert yourself early by asking for help, such as "I've had the kid(s) all day, can you have them for an hour/read the bedtime story/feed them/change them/settle them, while I have a break as I am tired too?"

You both need a chance to recharge your batteries and have some head space to process what you have achieved that day or plan what you would like to achieve tomorrow.

You will need to make time for self-care such as booking a trip to the hairdressers, nail bar, spa or reading a good book, the latest news in the papers or making a phone call to a friend. You need to keep in touch with people who know your former self, as this will remind you that you are an individual human as well as a mother.

Planning

Have a plan. Is your partner taking time out to focus on your child? Are you taking time out to focus on your child? Bear in mind if you have been a career woman up until now, mixing with your peers and customers, you will find it very difficult to be at home alone with a non-speaking, demanding baby human.

Added to this, you will have your new baby to look after, alongside all the relentless day time manual labour of changing nappies, washing up, cooking, keeping the house clean, shopping, organising your new life and finding out about and attending baby clubs, to meet other mums and have some adult company.

You will also have the night-time challenges of breast or bottle feeding, nappy changing, finding a dummy under the cot while having disturbed sleep throughout.

Your new life, with a young baby who seems to cry, poop and eat all day, may not be what all the advertisements, films and baby books say that it will be!

In addition, you may be iron deficient at best or recovering from a difficult labour, with complications for you and/or your new baby, so lacking in energy, leaving you feeling weak and tired.

Or you may be suffering from post-natal depression as your hormones fluctuate and you feel overwhelmed. If this is the case, you should talk to your health visitor who will have experience and know how to help you,

Be sure to make an hour slot for yourself each day, to reward yourself for all your hard work, so that you can recharge and do something for your own self-care.

There are a lot of tasks to do to maintain a home, a garden, a career and a social life. When you add children to the mix, you can see how it gets so much more complex.

Therefore, your own time, dreams and thoughts are reduced, step by step, to a full-time schedule of looking after others and effectively becoming a martyr to motherhood, with the only accepted break of a spa day once a year to re-enforce the idea that you are the lucky one.

In modern times, we have been socialised into believing that no-one can look after a child like their mother can, when actually in 'the good old days' there were phrases like 'it takes a village to raise a child'. It was understood that a mother could not do 'everything'.

Added to this, mothers these days have extra pressures put on them. As well as managing their home, their career and sorting out the best school for their children, they are now expected to research and find a range of after school activities from football to French, to pay for them, to get the kit, to drop off, to pick up, to keep up with the administration, to buy thank you cards and gifts and arrange end of year parties. It can be overwhelming.

The standards expected of modern women with phrases like 'Tiger Mom' and 'Helicopter Parenting' have increased exponentially, as well as being expected to bring in a good wage to the household, women still continue to have responsibility for 99% of the childcare so are under more pressures than ever before.

How many times have you tried to concentrate on your role, working from home and have become distracted by the many pulls on your attention? For example, a message from the school to add more money to the school dinner money account, signing a form for a school trip, then receiving a call from school as your child has forgotten their PE kit.

You then have to find the password on the dashboard (if it's not remembered for you), go to the bank app to check the funds are there, then put in the password, the card number, your name, expiry date and three-digit code. You then click here, there and everywhere until you forget what you were doing in the first place. You then have to breathe and somehow return to a deep focus mode to continue to do your job.

Moving from multi-tasking to deep dive concentration is exhausting. And if you are working from home, you then have to contend with the banging going on from next door's renovation works or the police siren going off or road work drilling. Minutes and hours can be lost trying to multi-task and enable everyone else to function. Argh!

The expectations on fathers, however, are completely different. They can continue to have their fun/make a baby and if not named on the birth certificate can happily skip away without a care in the world, without guilt, blame or shame.

Fathers can have many children to many women without a concern for their reputation, when in fact, they have often abandoned the mother at her most vulnerable, leaving her and an innocent baby. Take our recent Prime Minister and Presidents who were still voted in as acceptable leaders of the country, despite having denied the paternity of children from their past partners.

What message does this send to our country and culture about what is acceptable as a father or mother today?

If a woman went around having sex, getting pregnant, giving birth, abandoning the child and then moving on to the next partner, how would we view her? There would be public outcry, shaming, retribution and governmental penalties I am sure.

Once a woman has a child she has to act in a certain way or face judgement.

When she meets friends in the street, they no longer ask how she is but how the family is, as the polite form of address. No matter what she may be feeling she is not asked, after being seconded to her partner, she is 'thirded' to her family as they become the focus of conversation.

Therefore, her identity and individuality are further erased.

Imagine this for a new mother. Despite a new-found role of intense pressure with little sleep and 24/7 responsibilities, exhaustion of 2/3/4 hourly feeds throughout the day and night, of financial pressures and uncertainties and changes in relationships with her family, she has to change her routine, her friends and mostly reassess her hard-earned job. Her circumstances have changed, her body has changed (both inside and outside) her clothes have changed and her living conditions have changed.

Her budget and spending power has changed, so her spending habits have to change, her role in the home, her spontaneity and ability to leave the home is curtailed and her minute-by-minute routine has changed completely. She is now on call 24/7, throughout the day and throughout the night, with little regard for herself.

Her daily, weekly, monthly and yearly plans are changed. In fact, every area of her life is changed irrevocably forever.

If she had complications before, during or after the birth and has to recover fully, then she has additional pain and worry to endure, which is in fact most women, in my experience.

Then she has to enter a whole new culture where attending every post-natal appointment, children's club, feeding the family and maintaining the home is normalised, with no acknowledgement or thanks by leaders or society, of how much women support the economy with their unpaid and crucial work.

Women's bodies are turned inside out in childbirth and their former identity is virtually erased, so it is no wonder that they question who they are and what they have become.

Have YOU experienced this?

As a new mum I cooked meals from scratch, using the latest information about the most nutritious foods. I flick flacked between Jamie Oliver's latest bible, Mediterranean recipes and the odd mild curry (as the kids wouldn't eat the spicy foods I loved). I also couldn't handle much alcohol anymore, as after one hangover with a small child, I knew there was no way I could manage a headache and a toddler ever again, so again your lifestyle has to change.

Some parents have to leave their jobs due to the high cost of childcare, or lack of support from family. Therefore, it means that half the educated and skilled workforce are overnight reassigned to mindless, thankless and unpaid repetitive work.

If you have a new baby, you will no doubt experience sleepless nights and waking up every 2, 3 or 4 hours to breastfeed the baby. Then the next day you have to carry on as normal.

You have to feed the family so have to think of appropriate meals, provide food, prepare food, set the table, feed child(ren), clean up afterwards, wash up, clean tabletops, mop floors, fill the bin, empty the bin, dispose of the rubbish, feed yourself and make a hot drink (but often drink it cold).

Then dress the child(ren) - provide clothes, prepare clothes, choose clothes, put on clothes, take off clothes (more than once a day), put on clean clothes, take off dirty clothes etc.

If you are intelligent and educated and have read Cosmopolitan or any other magazine proclaiming that "you can have it all" then you must quash everything you have learned, to survive the daily grind.

The tactics you would employ to torture a prisoner are sleep deprivation, removal of familiar surroundings, imprisonment and repetitive labour, yet mothers do these tasks every day, weary, worn down, moulded and Motherhooded ©2024 with little chance of escape.

Having gone through it twice, it is only many years later that I can see the helicopter view of how busy and intense it was. Women are socialised to suppress their own needs and then acquire a long list of low-level jobs for the family and home. Feeding your child is urgent but giving yourself a 5 minute break and drinking a luke warm cuppa is near impossible until they are about 6 years old.

Thankfully, the intensity of Motherhood reduces when children go to school but the administration and school visits continue and this is mainly planned and managed by the mother who has historically been off work on maternity leave and so it seems to continue to be 'her role'.

By the time the children go to secondary school, the management, planning and administration has been done by the mother for over a decade, as well as the weight of physical, mental and emotional support for each child.

When your children go to high school, they need less daily practical support, but then you or your parents are older and can get sick or have health issues. Societally, it is usually the woman again who takes on the burden of caring duties.

This is akin to a middle management position as there is the pressure from above and below (managing parents and children) inside and outside the home. This is a lot of stress on the woman, again for no pay, so it is generally unseen and unaccounted for, but it is in fact a heavy burden that is both time consuming and tiring physically and emotionally.

Added to this, as a woman you may also experience the mental, physical and emotional effects of your hormones, as their levels plummet! In the next chapter I introduce the changes that come with the menopause.

Ideas to Action

① Were you prepared for motherhood?

② How did your life change?

③ Did you know your life would change this much before children?

④ Has your partner's daily life changed?

⑤ Can you still prioritise yourself after children?

⑥ Do you find it easy or hard?

⑦ Do you feel guilty or glad to have a break?

⑧ Do you get what you need/want?

⑨ Does your partner get what they need/want?

⑩ Do your children get what they need/want?

Empowering Actions

1. Discuss all the new tasks with your partner.

2. Plan how you will rest breaks in the day and evening, as parenting is hard work.

3. Make a plan to have fun each day.

4. How has your partner's life changed post children?

5. Open the conversation and discuss it with your friends.

6. Discuss if you are enabling poor fatherhood.

7. Are expectations the same for mothers?

8. What are you going to do about it?

9. Give yourself positive self-talk, such as "I did well to arrange a fair allocation of jobs today."

10. Pat yourself on the arm while you say it loud, for positive reinforcement.

CHAPTER 18

Menopaused ©2024

THERE ARE MANY CHANGES ahead in menopause but did you know that peri-menopausal symptoms can begin up to 10 years before full menopause? It is a slow process that often only makes sense in hindsight and is different for every woman.

The undeniable inconsistencies and lack of education about the menopause and women's issues in general, have fired up menopausal women today, as it is part of a whole matrix of issues that are unique to women and largely ignored.

On the plus side, this can be seen as a new chapter and a chance to create a new identity and start afresh as simultaneously your children are becoming more independent and may have fled the nest.

Personally, I feel re-ignited, with a new sense of urgency, so it's not all bad. However, this phase has also made me frustrated, angry and agitated. A voice deep inside me is rearing up its beautiful self, like a lionesses' roar (as per Katy Perry).

I am listening to this inner voice and channelling it as I grow in strength and energy. It is deeply personal and deeply universal and I hope to re-ignite and unite other women's passions and freedoms to create a better life for womankind.

Signs and Symptoms

The Fawcett Society's Report, 'Menopause in the Workplace' (2022) found that 77% of women experience very difficult symptoms which affect them in the workplace. Including:

- Sleepless nights
- Hot flushes
- Memory lapses
- Lack of focus
- Mood swings

These are all due to a huge drop in their oestrogen, progesterone and testosterone hormone levels and perhaps a lack of minerals and vitamins.

Added to this, the rise of cortisol levels in comparison, may leave you feeling more anxious and stressed. Working class women are said to suffer more and they say:

Society's silence on these issues is a scandal.

As these levels decrease and increase in your blood stream, you may feel out of control and not 'yourself'.

If this is how you feel, what can you do to help yourself?

It could also be exacerbated by the realisation that you are in a later stage of life. You may feel dissatisfied with where you are or want to change your lifestyle.

You may realise that you have so much more to do in life and so much more to give and want to start a new chapter in your life.

The Good News

You can now channel that energy and extra time into forging a new mission in your life, be it in a career or in your personal life. Hurray!

I found that I really was getting frustrated and less patient with those around me and once I got over this initial feeling of agitation, not knowing what I wanted and why, I turned it round positively and thought you know what? I may not have a lot of time left on this planet, so what's to lose!?

If you have always wanted to climb a mountain or jump out of a plane, then the world is yours. This is your chance to forge a new identity. Therefore, it can also be a very exciting time.

Simultaneously, your children may go to secondary school and do not want to be seen with you at the school gates anymore. Or you might find yourself with an 'empty nest' when your children have left home. They will become more independent and leave you with extra hours per day when you used to do the school runs.

Whatever situation you find yourself in, you can make up for lost time and be on a mission to do something for yourself.

Perhaps you want to channel that extra time and energy into giving back to the community? You could volunteer on a weekly basis in one of the ever-growing charity shops that pop up everywhere.

I can personally vouch that this is a rewarding way of spending your time, meeting a variety of new people, finding out what is going on in the community and learning new skills. It also makes you realise how lucky you are in life.

If you have a special charity that is close to your heart, you may wish to run a marathon (dressed as a chicken if you so please) and all in the interests of charity, of course.

You also have a lot of experience to pass on to the world and you could see it as your duty to pass on this knowledge and wisdom to the next generation, so they have the benefit of learning from your (joyful or painful) experiences.

You could even do a course. Have you always secretly wanted to a do a degree in English literature, or learn to swim? Now is the time to think about what you want to do and do it.

If you want to learn a new skill then you can build your skill set, gain knowledge and meet new people, which in turn will increase your confidence.

Mixing with other women in similar situations could give you companions who understand you and can support you in this phase and later on in life.

Finally, exercise has been proven to counteract the fluctuations of hormones, so running, walking, playing tennis, football, badminton or taking a dance class would be beneficial for your fitness levels and emotional wellbeing. You could tone up while you enjoy yourself and manage any stress in a natural way.

The menopause not only affects you but also the people you live with in your home. They will notice the changes in your moods and temperament and may feel upset or confused by your behaviour.

You need to communicate your feelings when you are calm as well as angry so that you can make a plan and get some sympathy for the changes you are going through.

In the next chapter I will discuss how men can get involved and support their life partners.

Ideas to Action

1. How do you feel?
   _____
   _____
   _____

2. Have you been affected by peri-menopause?
   _____
   _____

3. Have you been affected by menopause?
   _____
   _____

4. Has your partner been affected by peri-menopause or menopause?
   _____
   _____

5. Has your family been affected by peri-menopause or menopause?
   _____
   _____

6. What symptoms are you experiencing?
   _____
   _____

7. Do you need the support of other females of the same age?
   _____
   _____

8. Could you talk about your feelings and concerns?
   _____
   _____

9. What would be helpful to you?
   _____
   _____

10. What isn't helpful to you?
    _____
    _____

Actions to Empower

(1) Identify any symptoms you are experiencing.

_____

_____

_____

_____

_____

_____

_____

(2) Which friends can you contact to gain mutual support and advice?

_____

_____

_____

_____

_____

_____

(3) Make an appointment with your GP to discuss.

(4) Arrange for a full blood test to find out your progesterone, oestrogen and testosterone levels.

(5) Ensure you are taking multi-vitamin supplements so that your hormones are absorbed effectively.

(6) If you need HRT, then start taking it, as it can take a few months to take effect.

(7) Assess if HRT is working for you, make notes of how you feel and any changes in your body or moods.

(8) If HRT is not working effectively for you, make an appointment with your GP until it does.

(9) Give yourself positive self- talk, such as, "I have achieved .... today."

(10) Pat yourself on the arm while you say it loud, for positive reinforcement.

CHAPTER 19

To Our Male Partners

FEMINISM HAS HAD SOME criticism over the years, but personally I think all humans would benefit from a world of equality. Here's some thoughts I'd like to suggest to our male partners.

Men have nobly taken on the burden of earning the majority of the family's income in most families and if this is you, then you should be appreciated and thanked for it.

Chances are you would also appreciate more connection with your partner. Domestic slavery is not innate, fun or sexy for women. If your partner is spending most of her waking hours washing, ironing, cooking and cleaning, to the point of exhaustion, then why not lighten her load?

Men's Roles in Partnerships

It is also a system where men would rather die from suicide or a heart attack brought on by stress, than admit they have emotional needs, so we must change society to share the load in terms of childcare, financial responsibility and living a balanced life.

Men should be able to spend time with their children, communicate, show they care, give practical support and really get in touch with their 'emotional side', a side where they can talk it out if they are overwhelmed or in trouble and ultimately get help in terms of mental, emotional or practical support.

There is no shame in showing that you have emotions, although it takes courage. Men have it hard too in their own way.

How much happier could you both be if you could re-energise after work and get to come down from the stresses of the day, by chopping some vegetables and creating a gastro masterpiece?

It's strange that the two main Saturday cooking shows are hosted by men, although women do 80% of the cooking in real life.

If your partner cooks dinner three times a week and you cook dinner three times a week, then you can get a takeout, a ready meal, go out for dinner (if funds allow) or get the kids to make it on the seventh day. If you have a few children, then they can do a day each depending on their ages. Cooking is a vital skill for them to learn and they will then appreciate you more when a meal is cooked for them.

Thanks to companies like Hello Fresh for doing the thinking, planning and delivering, we may be able to breathe a sigh of relief that at least a couple of meals are sorted and as we do, our shoulders can go down slightly from the high, tense state they were in before. I hate cooking and when I say that I mean I am bored to death by the whole process. Chances are you or your partner might be too.

If you rebalanced tasks, it could mean a new phase in your life where you are able to reconnect, share the load and do fun things together, not just the mundane jobs of running the home.

Mumsnet is an app where mums can vent their frustrations anonymously and write about what's happening in their lives. One of these recent posts bemoaned the fact that when a partner does a job around the house he says, "I've washed the dishes FOR YOU" which shows an outdated attitude that jobs in the home are 'women's work'. Needless to say, this doesn't go down well with the mums of Mumsnet and rightly so.

Do you find yourself doing this or thinking like this? If so, you need to modernise your thinking, especially if you have daughters, or sons, for that matter.

IT'S A WIN-WIN!

Women need to feel loved and respected inside and outside the home for them to be in the right place to give back. If you give a little, in terms of energy and thoughtfulness and take responsibility for any jobs in the home or in childcare, then you will get a lot back.

Take it from me, it is not sexy for a woman to be enslaved in the kitchen. Would you want your daughters stuck in the kitchen? No? Why not?

So why is it acceptable for your partners to take on this load, often frustrated and unappreciated? It's no wonder she is often fed up.

How would you feel in this position if the role was reversed?

Here are the steps taken before a meal is put on the table:

a) Work out the budget.
b) Check cupboards/fridge/freezer to see what you already have.
c) Plan meals for the week.
d) Make shopping list taking into account family likes/dislikes/allergies/intolerances.
e) Travel to the supermarket.
f) Park the car.
g) Find coin and collect trolley.
h) Walk into supermarket.

i) Check labels for good deals.
j) Check items are not damaged before putting in trolley.
k) Walk up and down supermarket aisles.
l) Tick items off the list.
m) Go to the till.
n) Put food onto conveyor belt.
o) Take food off conveyor belt and sort into correct bags.
p) Purchase food.
q) Lift food from trolley into car.
r) Get into car and drive home.
s) Put food away in correct place - fridge, freezer and various cupboards.
t) Prepare the meal by taking out of wrapping and chopping.
u) Cook the meal at the right temperature for the right amount of time.
v) Set the table.
w) Serve the meal.
x) Wash and dry the dishes or load the dishwasher and switch it on.
y) Put the dishes away in the correct drawers and cupboards.

$a+b+c+d+e+f+g+h+i+j+ k +l +m+n+o+p+q+r+s+t+u+v+w+x+y$
$= Z$ (Paying)

Ask yourself:

- Is this an equal sum?
- Are the tasks of equal value?

- In what way can you help to equal the balance?
- What do you enjoy doing to prepare a meal?

Try working out your own equation. Could you take the initiative and order food online and get it delivered?

IT'S A WIN-WIN!

Better connection with your family

If you were to ring or text your mum, dad, sister or brother to ask them what they would like for their birthday, then the chances are that you would have a better connection with them. You've let them know that you've thought about them and that you value them and want to get them something they love or need. How lovely is that?

You will therefore be appreciated more and this positive connection with your family can then open the gate to other family connections such as having a meal, sharing a cake or even a night out, to celebrate with your loved ones.

IT'S A WIN-WIN!

Better connection with your children

You need to physically be there with your kids, not the big showy meal out, or the flash holiday. I mean the everyday, walk to the shop, talk about their day type of connection. You may have made a physical connection from your first skin to skin touch of father to baby when they were born, but it deepens your relationship if you continue your communication throughout their everyday lives, which is rewarding for you and them.

Again, a hug is a WIN-WIN and it's free!

Toxic Masculinity

We've heard a lot about toxic masculinity which is when men feel they have to act like a strong male without sharing their feelings or emotions which has been learned by men in our society, but is harmful in some way.

A combination of seen, spoken or unspoken words and actions combine to normalise how a male 'should' act. We all contribute to creating this masculine 'ideal' by encouraging or voicing what is typically acceptable male behaviour and what is not. You have the power to change this by opening up and talking about your feelings with your friends and relatives.

I have seen this 'ideal' change over the years from the way 'real' men were 'supposed to' behave in the 1970s. You only have to look at old James Bond movies to see the idealised behaviour for males and the idealised behaviour for females. James Bond often tried to seduce women (as a thank you for saving their lives) or they his, before trying to murder him!

The casual misogyny is almost jaw dropping as we look back and may feel outraged by how women were casually cast aside and seen as a prize to be 'had' after a successful mission.

Now that we are in more enlightened times, these films seem outdated and outrageous and clearly demonstrate the (male) writer or director enacting his own fantasies, under the guise of film making. You may see them as funny, rude, outrageous, sickening or downright offensive today, but back then it was the 'norm' of how a man could and should act, as James Bond was sold as the 'hero' that women adored and men wanted to be.

Looking back, it must have been difficult for boys and men to look at Mr Bond behaving like the alpha male. He had to be handsome, fit, witty, clever, cool under intense pressures, smooth, super smart, drive the best cars, have the latest tech gadgets (and be able to use them like a pro within 30 seconds). He also had to be physically fit, tanned, toned, have even white teeth, wear smart suits/dinner jackets and risk his life on a minute-by-minute basis.

We all contribute to normalising the acceptable behaviours of males and females and I am ashamed to say that I too have placed pressure on males if they have acted outside the construct of masculinity that I have in my own head. Of course, we are all thinking and feeling humans.

Just last weekend I went to London and sat at a table with my friend. As we caught up with what had been going on in our lives and our relationships, we felt free and relaxed at our table, had a few cocktails and a few dances.

At the next table were three men in their 30s, also drinking a range of cocktails, some with flames on top, some in mock wooden coconuts, containing liquids that were pink, green and blue. I was surprised to see this and said, "What the heck are you doing drinking cocktails?" They replied, "because we like them!" Fair enough.

In my experience growing up, the males in my world would not be seen drinking cocktails, or happily dancing around with their male friends. These men were harmless, they were having fun and who was I to comment on their choice of drink?

I spoke to another couple during the night too. I remarked that I hadn't seen a group of males drinking cocktails before and asked the man would he drink a cocktail? He was muscly, tall, handsome and a police officer of around 30 years old. To my surprise, he said yes as he had a sweet tooth.

It seems that having sweet drinks with colourful accessories is no longer the domain of the female, males can also enjoy them and long may it last.

Mental Health

Thankfully, sportsmen such as Ian Wright are leading the way by taking part in documentaries, sharing their personal stories of when they were young and being vulnerable when they open up about the mental struggles they have been through.

Hopefully this will lead to more men opening up, rather than putting up and shutting up, about their own emotional and mental health struggles. I hope there will be less suicides in young males and a massive shift in changing our culture to what is and what is not appropriate and acceptable in order to be masculine.

Men weren't taught the tools of talking about their feelings, so can find it difficult, if not impossible, to even start a conversation with their partners, never mind their male friends who ironically are probably struggling with the very same issues.

With this in mind, New Zealand started a charity called Menzshed for men to join, open up, support, learn skills and look after their mental and emotional health. This has been successfully rolled out across the country. Perhaps the men in the rest of the world need this too?

Wouldn't it be better to show and give support to each other, males and females? Surely it is a win-win, sharing each other's loads and mixing up the list of humdrum chores, communicating more and reaching a deeper level of understanding and appreciation on both sides?

Misogyny

This is a collective term for when men diminish, stereotype, describe or treat women as 'less than'. It sometimes brings up how men think about women and what is normal behaviour to them. For example, jokes or references like 'my wife is a nag' shifts the blame onto the woman (for her 'behaviour') whereas the woman would not have to repeat herself if the partner recognised the problem themselves or did the task when first asked.

It's linked to women still being perceived as having responsibility for the management of the home and the children and it permeates society in many ways. Whether it's the limitations put on women, not because of their abilities, but because of the role that is expected of them in society, individual by individual.

It is a culture that is embedded and accepted in the world today. In reality, women are generally too tired to shout or to bring their struggles to the attention of the world, as they are concentrating on their family's survival.

However, we should be focusing on the bigger picture of how to improve society for our generation and the next, for the benefit of all humankind.

We need to shift out of our binary modes too. Sexuality is on a spectrum, we are not one or the other. We also need to get out of the black and white way of thinking.

Humans are not black or white but come in all shades, sizes, shapes and abilities. Our skin comes in shades from bluey white to beige to pink to brown to black. It's a glorious rainbow.

The cultures we all come from have advantages and disadvantages and offer us different perspectives. The cliché "it would be boring if we were all the same" is true. We all need to listen more and understand more.

Thankfully, sexuality and gender are now recognised as less binary with a recognition of the LGBTQ+ communities and their unique perspectives, slowly but surely.

Capitalism

In the western world, this is the construct we live in today. We focus on the numbers, whilst disregarding the value or the feelings and the actions that are borne for the good of us all. Women too are carrying this load individually and collectively.

We are living in a quantitative not a qualitative society, where greed and selfishness (to the exclusion of human qualities like kindness and nurture) are celebrated above all.

This is not my idea of success and ultimately is unrewarding. We are social beings who seek affirmation and approval from our tribe. If our peers start to value and endorse qualities such as wisdom, experience and collaboration, then people would start to change from wanting the latest car, to wanting to listen, empathise and collaborate for deeper connection and fulfilment.

Misandry

You may not have heard of it but this is the word for dislike, contempt or ingrained prejudice against men.

Compare this with the name for those people who hate women and I have to confess as an educated person, I had to look it up to see if there was such a word.

This could be because it isn't a pervasive attitude, or it is in such small pockets of society that it hasn't become mainstream, but what I do know is that it is not nearly as big a threat to society that misogyny is.

For the record I believe we are all individuals and no one behaviour is representative of a whole gender, but we do see patterns in life which are useful to identify.

In this book I've sectioned male and female behaviours as this is the mainstream experience of today but I believe we all need to collaborate and communicate more, recognising and utilising the best qualities of all genders, to ensure acceptance and progression in society.

What can you do to contribute to this progress?

Ideas to Action

1. Could you do more around the home?

2. Could you do more with your children?

3. How do you feel when you connect with your partner?

4. How do you feel when you connect with your children?

5. Could your friends do more in their homes?

6. Could your friends do more with their children?

7. Do you think they might regret NOT spending more time with their children.

8. Could you chat more openly about your feelings with your friends?

9. Could you chat more openly about your feelings with your family?

10. How could they change this?

Actions to Empower

1. Call a friend(s) today and tell them you like/love or miss them.

2. Arrange to meet a friend(s).

3. Meet up with a friend and tell them if you need help or support.

4. Arrange to go out for the day with your child, one on one.

5. Arrange to go out for the day with your other child, one on one.

6. Spend quality time with your partner and let her know how you feel.

7. Spend quality time with your child in the home and have a chat to keep communications open.

8. Spend quality time with your other children, listen and let them know how you feel about them.

9. Give yourself positive self-talk, such as "I have done a great job listening to my child today."

10. Pat yourself on the arm while you say it out loud, for positive reinforcement.

CHAPTER 20

Where Next?

AS A MIDDLE-CLASS female in the UK, I realise that I am very fortunate. I have the education, the experience and the ability to see patterns in my life and that of my friends, family, acquaintances and peers.

I see women everywhere soothing and supporting and doing the repetitive work that keeps their family, their town, their country and their world safe, but their wombs have been weaponised against them, consistently keeping them in the interior world of the home and out of the exterior world where decisions are made and power is gained.

Therefore, I feel it is our responsibility as women, to push forward and motivate other females who are struggling for survival on a mental, emotional and physical basis, every minute of every day.

This book is part feminist theory, part personal journey and part social commentary, as I want you to be inspired as an individual to take action.

I haven't got all the answers yet, but I want you to join me on this journey, for us all to live our best lives, ignite our passions and achieve our true potential.

After decades of learning to put yourself last in society, you are brainwashed to believe you are not even the most important person in your own life.

Women all over the world are putting on a brave face, wasting their precious time, collecting crumbs, wiping worktops and making magnificent meals, for it all to be invisible and un-noticed.

And parts of our identity are systematically erased one by one, as we go through women's 'rights of passage'.

No wonder we lose ourselves and find it hard to remember what we like, what we want and where we want to go in life.

Women are often undervalued by themselves and each other. We need to be reminded how unique, talented and wonderful we truly are.

If you admire someone who is clever or talented. Tell them. It will make a huge difference to their confidence and self-belief and who knows where this confidence will take them?

We could all benefit by listening and collaborating with a greater pool of talent. Did you know that talent scouts are being sent all over Africa to find the best football players?

Why can't this be the case for every field, such as astrophysics, engineering or astrology? Imagine how far our knowledge would progress if half the population were not subjugated and oppressed, kept in kitchens or wiping worktops?

Society has us believe that hundreds of menial jobs are the responsibility of the woman of the house and as people pleasers, we have taken them on.

In the long term I know this system is going to fail as we get tired, frustrated and resentful. No-one wants this, especially the people who love us and live with us.

We need to communicate and delegate some of these jobs without guilt. If we are to reach our true potential, we must carve out time to pursue our own interests and maintain our individual identities.

This is NOT being selfish; this is for our long-term survival and provides role models for our children to aspire to.

Women are socialised to serve, soothe and 'keep the peace'. It can be difficult to maintain your individuality and independence as you are overlooked, downgraded and constrained within the restrictions and expectations of friends, family and society.

Imagine if all us women had a chat. The chat was not purely commiserating on our lot, but we had the head space to gather our collective ideas, the time to action those ideas and the energy to create a more balanced world where our partners took turns in the home, they might enjoy it, or be better at it!?

Male partners would also get a balance, where they had less pressure to earn the most and provide for their family, to always be the physically strong one, to keep their emotions hidden, being responsible for changing only the light bulbs and bins. They would have more time to reconnect with their children, family and friends.

Men and women are individual humans who have unique skills and attributes at any given time. Men often feel overburdened at work, whilst women now feel overburdened at home and at work too.

In my view, what most politicians put on their agenda is decided by the media or their own personal experiences. Generally, a 'he' decides where to put his energies, what to promote and what to put to the bottom of his list.

The News is miserable and oppressive and we feel powerless to help the hungry so switch off. Who decides this agenda and why? Where are the positive stories of good in the world? The balance is tipped towards reporting on more evil and hate.

As men are still the majority in government, what *men* think is important, takes priority, not what is important to women or families. This might explain why men like Putin are on a path of destruction.

Bad behaviour needs to be publicly called out and we need to take a stance collectively. It took 81 world class female footballers to go on strike before the President of the Spanish Football Association stood down for misogyny.

This is yet another example of how society sets men up (and keeps them) in positions of economic power and controls females.

- Who wins from this set up?
- Who gets the treats, the rewards, the power and the pay?
- Who loses from this set up?
- Who literally gets stuck with the crumbs?
- What can you do about it?

The pursuit of goals gives humans pleasure at a deep level. This is your body and mind propelling you to self-actualise and be the best you can be for the good of humanity. At times it may be difficult, but you will be so much more fulfilled to know that you at least tried.

Humans should not be separated by their gender, sexuality, race, religion or colour. Individuals are far more complex than that and the progression of humankind is now at stake. We need to work through a progressive agenda, one item at a time.

Caitlin Moran called for a "union for women" and this sounds like a great idea to me, but we need to start gaining strength individually first. We need to enable ourselves and each other.

Women have been fighting for freedom and respect for centuries and we need to keep pushing forward NOW.

The frustration is that women are partly responsible for this set up. We have enabled this patriarchal system of norms and beliefs, by staying silent and not speaking up. We have been well and truly #Womanhooded.

I don't know about you, but when I think about standing up for myself, if it's for me I feel selfish for asking, but if it's for my children I can be strong and fearless and will stop at nothing to save and prioritise them to get what they need.

Women need to step out of the passenger seat we are often put in. It can be a scary, unpredictable and bumpy ride but we need to take control.

I see women everywhere who are afraid to look up or stand up, we need to be role models for ourselves and the next generation. There is power in the spoken and written word.

We women need to stop wasting most of our time 'looking' or 'being' in the interior world and more time 'doing' in the 'exterior' world, to reach our full potential. Society needs to change to support us.

Why are we prioritising handbags over homeless humans on the street? Hungry people are visiting food banks more than ever and wars and torture prevail.

Yet the present media set up capitalises on us spending all our precious time preening, pampering and comparing ourselves to false images. It is diverting us from real human interaction and progression.

We need action not eyeliner, muscles not mascara and ideas not eyeshadow.

There are big problems on this planet today. We should use our energies to conserve the earth, the people and the creatures who live on it. Do you have an idea to improve the world?

Trust me, you are more intelligent than you know and that voice inside you with an idea, a dream or an ambition is right. Listen to her.

It's very hard to take that first big step into the unknown, to step out of your comfort zone and see what you can achieve.

Take off your 'womanhood' and breathe in the fresh air, it's exhilarating!

If you could start with just one item. Take a deep breath (like you would in labour and breathe through the pain!), use your voice and start talking about this unfairness, and any other, with your friends and with your family. Make a list and action it to start changing it, one item at a time.

I invite you to join 51% of the population and empower yourself to make some positive changes in the world today. It's over to you to plan and decide your next steps and how you want your life to be.

If not you, who?

Ideas to Action

1. What do you think could improve the world for women?

2. Could you help towards this?

3. Could you start this campaign?

4. Could you contact a friend to make an action plan together?

5. How could your partner improve the world for men?

6. Could your partner start a campaign?

7. Could your partner contact a friend to make an action plan together?

8. Do you think the news today is depressing?

9. Who do you think makes the news agenda?

10. Do you think we should change what is reported on the news to get a balance of good and bad?

Actions to Empower

(1) Ring a friend and discuss how you could change the world for women?

(2) Ring a friend and arrange a meeting to discuss further.

(3) Have a chat with your partner and discuss your feelings about the world today.

(4) Have a chat with your partner about what makes you both happy.

(5) Have a chat with your partner about what makes you both sad.

(6) Have a chat with your partner about the news today.

(7) How could you start a campaign to gain a balanced view of the world?

(8) Share a good news story with your friends.

(9) Plan what you are going to do to be a positive role model for women.

(10) Do it!

Acknowledgements

I WOULD LIKE to honour my grandmother, Mary McDonnell, who was a huge influence on me growing up. She was the first in the street to get a TV and a divorce!

To Kathy Hill, my Mum, who is wise, strong, constant, a great listener and a trusted confidante. Thank you for everything you have done over the years, it's a lot!

To Su Hill, my Aunty who is a force of nature. She has the strength, determination and fortitude of an ox.

To Rosanna, you inspire me every day to be better. Your emotional intelligence, courage and strength are off the scale!

To Zoe, your maturity, intelligence and determination are undeniable. I admire you so much!

To Lucy and Laura, my cousins and pseudo sisters, for fun times and happy memories.

To my extended family, Chrissie, Christina, Janet, Kate, Michaela, Margaret and the next generation of strong women Mary, Lily, Isobel, Alexa, Natalie, Phoebe, Thea and Winnie.

To the strong role models I've met on the networking circuit including; Aga Mortlock, Alex McCann, Anna Barker, Ashley Costello, Beth Penfold, Catherine Sandland, Dani Wallace, Emma Guy, Jane Kenyon, Joanna Scott-Aspray, Jodie Salt, Kerry Daynes, Lisa Payne, Sarah E Pickles and Sue France.

To my friends Alison Shaffer, Andi Whittaker, Becky Graham, Carol Simpson, Collette Walsh, Diane Flanagan, Emma Beard, Emma Kay, Emma Wilson, Heather Barlow, Heidi Birkett, Jayne Bailey, Jeanette Yen, Jolly Cao, Joanna Wivell, Jonathan Chianca, Karen Steele, Leanne Davis, Lisa Payne, Lyndsey Holden, Rachel Badzire, Rachel Hardy and Tanya Wragg who along the way have been inspiring, empowering, funny, supportive, mad, bad and glad when I've needed them!

To the Divas who dance, thank you for your strong support!

Love to our New Zealand friends who became family to us and always will.

To the Women who did the school run from 2010 to today!

Last but definitely not least, to my partner Gerard, for your grit, determination, support and understanding, shouldering the huge responsibility of keeping the roof over our heads.

I am eternally thankful that I have you all in my life.

To my readers, you are living your one and only life, so reclaim it and keep in touch with your inner voice because she is *ALWAYS RIGHT.*

Much love, *Joanna x*

References and Further Reading

THESE BRILLIANT BRAINS AND superb writers have inspired me along the way.

The Beauty Myth by Naomi Wolf, *Chatto & Windus Ltd* (1990). She predicted a future where men would be under the same pressures as women. It came true.

The Bell Jar by Sylvia Plath, *Faber & Faber* (1963). Disturbing, revealing, genius semi-biographical story of an oppressed woman and her mental illness.

Black Feminist Thought: Knowledge, Consciousness, and the Politics of Empowerment by Patricia Hill Collins, Unwin Hyman, *(1990).* Her standpoint theory emphasised the perspective of African American women under oppression.

Britney Spears' Family Has Dark History of Locking Women Up Article in New York Times by Dana Kennedy, Oct 9, 2021 –https://nypost.com/ 2021/10/09/ britney-spears-family-has-dark-history-of-locking-women-up.

Cosmopolitan Magazine, various - as a regular reader, this magazine was responsible for me asking for a pay rise and 'wanting it all in life!'

The Cinderella Complex by Colette Dowling, *Pocket Books* (1982). Fantastic insight into how girls are socialised into believing they need their own "Prince" to save them - they don't!

Daring Greatly by Brené Brown, Gotham Books (2012). Thought leading book which explains that we need courage to be vulnerable which is perceived as a weakness but it can become a strength.

The *Decision Making Unit (DMU)* coined by Philip Kotler in Competitive Strategies for New Product Marketing over the Life Cycle, Management Science (1965). He identifies all the individuals involved in purchasing a product or service.

Every Woman's Lifeguide by Miriam Stoppard, *Tor Leisure Circle Ltd* (1982). A definitive guide on how to be a physically and emotionally happy woman throughout your life. Well ahead of her time in writing about menopause.

The Female Eunuch by Germaine Greer, *Flamingo* (1970). She challenged women's traditional role in society and gave a framework for the feminist movement.

The Feminine Mystique by Betty Friedan Penguin Modern Classics (1921). Insightful research into why women in 1950s America and today feel unfulfilled and are not becoming their true selves.

Feminist Words: New Vocabulary to Empower Yourself (4 March 2020) Sarah Luisa Santos, Babbel Magazine - Explaining Bropriating, Mansplaining and Manterrupting - https://www.babbel.com/en/magazine/feminist-vocabulary/

The *Gender Pay Gap in the UK* (Nov 2022), statistics from Office of National Statistics (ONS) website https://www.ons.gov.uk/employmentandlabourmarket/peopleinwork/earningsandworkinghours/bulletins/genderpaygapintheuk/2021

"The Male Gaze" Wikipedia (2023) identifies the feminist theory of how women are viewed in literature and art as viewed by a male heterosexuals eyes.

Menopause in the Workplace, Andrew Bazeley, Catherine Marren and Alex Shepherd, The Fawcett Society (2022)

How to recycle Makeup and Reuse your Beauty Products Properly, Christobel Hastings, Shannon Lawlor, Lottie Winter and Elle Turner (6 March 2023), Glamour Online.

Personal finance, the gender pay gap, the gender literacy gap & the gender investment gap (2022) by Holly Holland and Laura Pomfret from Financielle (financielle.co.uk)

How to Win Friends and Influence People by Dale Carnegie, Vermillion (2006). A classic book on how to understand and get on with people.

'Hygiene Factors' Theory in The Motivation to Work by Frederick Herzberg (1959). Demonstrates relationship of job tasks and satisfaction.

Inside Women's Magazines by Janice Winship, Pandora (1987). Critiques adverts and how they portray women in modern society including the Male Gaze.

Madonna: The Virgin Tour on video (1985) Sire Records - thank you for being strident, independent, visual and vocal.

Marilyn Monroe a Never-ending Dream compiled and edited by Guus Luijters (1986) Plexus Publishing Ltd.

"Men are afraid that women will laugh at them. Women are afraid that men will kill them". (1980) Margaret Atwood.

MumsNet - (2000-to date) to the founder Justine Roberts and each individual positive contributor! In a Covid world, you will never know how much you helped me feel part of a community of supportive women. Thank you.

The Personal is Political by Kara Rogers and Christopher J Kelly, Britannica Website (1 May 2017). This is also called 'the private is political' which is a slogan expressing a common belief among feminists that each woman's personal experience is a symptom of their political situation and the gender inequality that exists.

The Personal is Political (1969) and *Women of the World Unite* By Hanisch (carolhanisch.org).

The Power by Naomi Alderman, Little Brown & Co (2017). A genius and thought provoking dystopian book about a world where women react to the evil acts of males and use their newly found powers to gain control of society.

Queenagers by Eleanor Mills, Founder of noon.org.uk (December 2022) in collaboration with Accenture coined the term for educated, affluent and open-minded women oner 40 who outspend millennials by 250%.

The Secret by Rhonda Byrne, Simon & Schuster UK (2006). This book explains the law of attraction so that you can focus on realising your hopes and dreams.

Untamed by Glennon Doyle, The Dial Press (2020). Wow! Thank you for presenting an alternative world where a woman follows her heart and not what she has been taught to do by society. She is a visionary,

Violence Against Women and Girls: Action Plan by Cressida Dick, Metropolitan Police (May 2022). (https://www. met.police.uk).

Woman x Two: How to Cope with a Double Life by Mary Kenny, Hamlin Paperbacks (1979). Trailblazer writing about how women are expected to be twice as much as men in their home, with their family and in their working life to survive.

The Sociological Imagination by C Wright Mill, Pelican (1959). He argued that individual experiences are inextricably connected with the greater social and historical experience.

Further Viewing and Listening

Britney Vs Spears, Journalist Jenny Eliscu and film-maker Erin Lee Carr investigate Britney Spears' fight for freedom, Netflix (2021).

The Spice Girls - channel the energy or the words for whoever you want to be and use it as your soundtrack in life. I thank them for their drive, determination and using their voices - "Who do you think YOU are?!"

Spice Girls: How Girl Power Changed Britain, produced and directed by Vari Innes, Alice McMahon-Major, and

Jessica Ranja, Channel 4, (2021). Three part documentary covering the social importance of Girl Power.

Lady Boss, The Jackie Collins Story by Laura Fairrie - iPlayer (2021).

Look out for more books in the series

Menopaused © 2024
Motherhooded © 2024
Manhooded © 2024
Fatherhooded © 2024

Follow me on: *Instagram @iamjoannalambe*

Milton Keynes UK
Ingram Content Group UK Ltd.
UKHW022120030124
435425UK00017B/1127